BEAD SOUP

32 Projects Show What Happens When 26 Beaders Swap Their Stash

Lori Anderson

KB
KALMBACH BOOKS

Kalmbach Books
21027 Crossroads Circle
Waukesha, Wisconsin 53186
www.Kalmbach.com/Books

Published in 2012
16 15 14 13 12   1 2 3 4 5

Manufactured in the United States of America

ISBN: 978-087116-442-1
EISBN: 976-0-87116-749-1

Editor: Karin Van Voorhees
Art Director: Lisa Bergman
Illustrator: Kellie Jaeger
Photographer: William Zuback

Library of Congress Cataloging-in-Publication Data

Anderson, Lori, 1969-
   Bead soup : 32 projects show what happens when 26 beaders swap their stash / Lori Anderson ; [with contributions from multiple designers].

   p. : ill. (chiefly col.) ; cm.

   1. Beadwork—Patterns. 2. Beadwork—Handbooks, manuals, etc. 3. Jewelry making—Handbooks, manuals, etc. I. Title.

TT860 .A63 2012
745.594/2

CONTENTS

INTRODUCTION

It was the cat's fault. My beading table is generally very, very cluttered. My bead cabinet, on the other hand, is quite organized, with trays separated by color, then type. Gemstones have their own trays, while vintage beads are tucked away in individual boxes, hoarded for a later date. But my beading table? That's always chaotic.

So there I sat, completely happy, beading away, with glass, ceramic, and crystal beads all around me. I'd been busy for weeks, preparing for a show, and loose beads were all over the table. I was incredibly behind schedule and hadn't taken any time to put beads away as I finished with this bag or that strand, just scooting beads impatiently to the side as I plugged away. Around 2:00 a.m. I'd had enough, and staggered to bed without another look at my table.

That night, a cat fight arose.

I don't know who started it—Vernon or Max—but I'm fairly certain it was 22-lb. Vernon who swept across my beading table in the middle of the night. Twenty-two pounds is quite a lot of cat. So when I woke to start another day of marathon beading, I was stunned by what I found in my studio.

Beads everywhere. Beads overboard. Beads on the floor. Beads rolling from one room into another. And two cats looking at me with suspiciously innocent eyes as if to say, "What?"

With resignation, I grabbed a bowl and started picking up the beads. One after another went into the bowl, a hodge-podge of colors, shapes, sizes, and styles. When I was done, I looked down at a colorful mess of what could only be described as Bead Soup.

And an idea began to take shape.

Rather than sort hundreds of beads into their proper bags and boxes, I started linking them together onto charm chain to create a cornucopia of color and texture. I quickly realized Bead Soup made one heck of a cool charm bracelet. Bead Soup became a staple food on my bead table.

In December 2009, I read a post on ArtBeadScene.com about having a party where each guest brought strands of beads to trade. Since I live in a rural area, I'm hours away from any beading friends and rely upon the Internet to connect with other people who adore beads. Why not partner up people who'd never met to trade beads with each other and then ask them to make something with what they received? I hoped people would expand their horizons and stretch their skills. After all, who hasn't been in a rut before? I also wanted people to find more beading blogs and connect them with like-minded jewelry designers. All these ideas came together into one online event, and the Bead Soup Blog Party was born.

Suffice it to say, I had no idea what I'd started.

About this book

This book is written like a Bead Soup Blog Party. Twenty-six participants from 11 states and five countries either sent me beads or created jewelry with beads they received in the mail from others. You'll find a mix of styles, techniques, and of course, a huge selection of beads.

If you've got a little stringing experience, you'll be able to jump right into the projects and start creating. If you need to brush up on a few beading skills, turn to Basics on page 92 for directions for all the techniques you'll need to complete the projects in the book.

One important thing to remember as you follow the directions is don't worry too much if you can't find a specific bead. Just as these designers did, I encourage you to experiment, to dig through your forgotten stashes of beads, to trade with friends, and to explore bead stores for substitutions. Each project can be an amazing jumping-off point for your own brand of creativity, helping to develop your own style. Take a pinch of this, a teaspoon of that, and stir up your own unique and delicious bowl of Bead Soup.

I opened the first Bead Soup Blog Party sign-ups in December of 2010. In a few short days, I had over 80 participants. I paired up bloggers and laid down the rules. Each person had to send a pretty clasp, a focal, and some coordinating beads. The recipient would make something out of their beads and show it off on the Party day—a massive blog hop where the participants posted their creations on their blogs and visited all the other participants' blogs as well.

Each designer had to use the focal and the clasp, any or all of the coordinating beads, and any beads they wanted to add from their own stash. The hope? To help people think outside the box and work outside their normal comfort zone, pushing them into creative directions they may never have gone on their own.

Soup Goes Global

A side effect of the Bead Soup Blog Party was a fabulous surprise—it went global! Suddenly beaders from all around the world were asking to participate. Held twice a year, the Bead Soup Blog Party quickly grew to hundreds of participants from over 20 countries. Some people discovered new friends who lived just around the corner, while others discovered the joys of learning about new countries and the unique beads found there. Many people who felt isolated (just like I had) felt their world grow smaller through the party.

Social media became just as important a factor for the party as the beads. People who had never blogged before got the nerve to start a blog just to participate in the party and discovered a new outlet for their creativity. Veteran bloggers saw their page hits and followers increase. All participants discovered new blogs, leading to new Facebook and Twitter friends. As the number of participants continued to grow, so did their desire to stay connected on a regular basis, and so the Facebook group Bead Soup Cafe was created.

The Bead Soup Blog Party has become much more than a blog hop—it has become a community.

If you would like to join a Bead Soup Blog Party, visit lorianderson-beadsoupblogparty. blogspot.com. You can join the forum at beadsoupcafe.com. Parties are held twice a year and anyone from any country can join.

Welcome to the community!

Bead Soup Blog Party

Sept 17, 2011

5 continents
21 countries
362 participants

CHAPTER ONE
THE LEFTOVER BEAD METHOD

In my house, no bead goes unloved. I have a bowl on my table where the leftover beads from strands and bags get tossed. When the bowl is full, I start mixing it up, adding a bit of this and taking out some of that, to create a colorful, eclectic necklace or bracelet. It's amazing what leftover beads can become!

The following projects can be made with your leftovers bowl. Don't have a leftovers bowl? Oh my! Well, here's what you do. Put a bowl on your beading table and when you have a few beads left over from a project or a strand of beads, toss them into the bowl. Before long, you'll end up with a colorful blend that is so full of possibilities, you'll be making soup recipes for weeks.

Bead Soup Soup

Ingredients
Bead Soup used from Joanna Matuszczyk (Poland)
Choose random beads in a pleasing color palette to suit your personal style.
Here, I've used cape amethyst, blue lace agate, ruby agate, opalite, Czech
glass,amethyst, ceramic, chrysoprase, amazonite, crystal quartz, malachite,
jasper, sterling silver, and pewter.

Soup's on!

These first projects are more free-flowing
than the rest in the book. They're meant to
show how one bowl of beads can turn into
many different pieces of jewelry. In addition,
I'll share my thoughts on wire gauge, bead
placement, texture, and metal choices. Are
you ready?

This long necklace takes advantage of gemstones, glass, Bali silver, and ceramic beads. Its length lets you showcase favorite leftover beads or those saved from special purchases. Each bead unit is a wrapped-loop link, making it easy for you to move the beads around your workspace, getting the colors, sizes, and textures just right. Smaller beads can be stacked to form longer links to mix better with your larger bead choices.

Connecting wrapped-loop links with jump rings gives the flexibility of moving beads around on a whim, and if you decide you like a different pattern or colorway better, you can easily open and close jump rings and exchange links. I've also found that long necklaces flow better when connected with jump rings instead of wiring the units directly together.

Balance is important in whatever jewelry you make. Space larger beads so they don't weigh down one section, and try different textures with different shapes of beads. While this piece was made with oxidized wire, you can make it with any color metal.

For the earrings, I cut a few links of the aluminum bracelet chain (page 9) and used two matching ceramic beads from the Bead Soup. Instead of commercial spacers, I opened and closed one jump ring through two closed jump rings to form a simple love knot.

A bracelet can start with a large stone, as with this 30x20mm jasper rectangle. For larger beads, I like to use a thicker wire gauge (here, 18-gauge) to complement the size of the bead. To balance the weight of the stone, I added a fringed chain with 10mm links and started wire-wrapping a multitude of green, purple, and amber beads to the chain with 20-gauge headpins.

This bracelet is similar in style to the first necklace, but takes advantage of lightweight aluminum chain to make a double-strand bracelet without much bulk or weight. Mix gemstones and glass. Combine multiple beads on one unit. Make the bead units with wrapped loops first, then connect them with jump rings. Because this bracelet is more delicate, I used 3mm jump rings and 22-gauge wire for the beaded section.

Bead Soup beading doesn't have to mean random bead placement. These malachite earrings show how to work with leftover pairs.

Tip When working with small 4mm beads as dangles, I like to complete all the dangles first, string them onto half a wrapped loop, and THEN complete the wrapped loop. This method works especially well for me when I want to make a very full cluster. If you prefer to wire wrap the smaller beads onto the finished loop, a set of fine-nose chainnose pliers comes in handy to fit into the smaller spaces.

Soup of the Day

Ingredients
Bead Soup used from Heather Powers (Michigan)
40mm Vintaj brass water lily component (P275)
24mm blue, brown, and white polymer clay lentil bead, Heather Powers
18mm square brass toggle
4 14mm blue dyed chalcedony smooth rondelles
3 12mm blue, brown, and white polymer clay rondelle beads, Heather Powers
21 8mm teal Czech glass melon beads
6-in. (15cm) strand 12mm gray keshi pearls

Beads used from Cindy Wimmer's Pantry:
5 18mm bronze flower bead caps
10 10mm bronze flower bead caps
18 8mm brass scalloped bead caps
50 8° bright teal frosted transparent seed beads
5 10mm smooth smoky quartz rounds
20 in. (51cm) 20-gauge oxidized brass or bronze wire
6 in. (5cm) brass rolo chain with 5mm links
5½ in. (1.3cm) brass oval link chain with 6x10mm links
15 2-in. (5cm) brass headpins
18 in. .019 or .014 beading wire (must fit through pearls)
4 crimp tubes (sterling silver or brass)
4 brass crimp covers

Utensils
-Roundnose pliers
-Chainnose pliers
-Flatnose pliers
-Crimping pliers
-Wire cutters
-Metal shears
-Metal file

Don't you love having choices—like the soup of the day—when you go to a restaurant? This necklace, with its distinctive strands, brings to mind a soup menu, with three very different tastes and textures to delight the palette.

Recipe

1 Using metal shears, cut the 40mm Vintaj brass water lily component at the corners to create four separate links. File the cut edges until smooth.

Tip Always file in one direction— do not use a sawing motion.

2 Cut a 4-in. (10cm) piece of wire. Make a wrapped loop. String three polymer clay rondelles. Make the first half of a wrapped loop. Attach a link from Step 1 and complete the wraps.

3 Cut a 2¾-in. (1.9cm) piece of oval 6x10mm link chain. Open an end link and attach to the the water lily link. Close the link. Open the remaining end link and string through the hole in the toggle square. Close the link.

4 Cut a 4-in. piece of wire. Make a wrapped loop and string the polymer clay lentil bead. Make a wrapped loop above the bead, connecting it to a link from Step 1.

5 Repeat Step 3, substituting the toggle bar at the end of the chain.

Strand 1 (outer)

6 Cut a 3-in. (7.6cm) piece of wire. Make a wrapped-loop link with a chalcedony rondelle bead. Make a total of four chalcedony links.

7 On a headpin, string an 8mm melon bead and a 10mm brass flower bead cap. Make the first half of a wrapped loop. Make a total of 10 dangles.

8 On a headpin, string a 10mm smoky quartz round and a 16mm brass flower bead cap. Make the first half of a wrapped loop. Make a total of five dangles.

9 Cut two 8-link and three 7-link pieces of rolo chain. Opening and closing the ends of the chain as you would jump rings, connect: 8-link piece, chalcedony link, 7-link piece, chalcedony link, 7-link piece, chalcedony link, 7-link piece, chalcedony link, 8-link piece.

10 Open the link on one end of an 8-link piece of chain and attach it to the wrapped loop of the polymer clay rondelle unit. Open the link on one end of a 8-link piece of chain and attach it to the wrapped loop of the polymer clay lentil bead.

Tip If you ended up with your middle three necklace strands too short, adjust the final length by adding a longer piece of oval chain at the ends.

11 Attach the loop of a smoky quartz flower dangle to the center of a piece of rolo chain. Complete the wraps. Skip two or three links on each side and string a Czech glass flower dangle. Complete the wraps. Repeat for all the pieces of rolo chain.

Strand 2 (middle)

12 Cut a 9-in. (23cm) piece of beading wire. String a crimp bead, the wrapped loop of the polymer clay bead link, and go back through the crimp. Crimp and cover with a brass crimp cover.

13 String: five 8º seed beads, a brass scalloped bead cap, a Czech glass melon bead, and a bead cap. Repeat until the strand is within 2 in. (5cm) of Strand 1. End with five 8ºs.

14 String a crimp bead and the wrapped loop of the polymer clay beads. Go back through the crimp. Crimp and cover with a brass crimp cover.

Strand 3 (inner)

15 Repeat Step 12.

16 String an 8mm Czech glass melon bead, 18 pearls, and an 8mm melon.

17 Repeat Step 14. Strands 2 and 3 will be approximately the same length.

Ladle It Out!

By Lori Anderson (Maryland)

Ingredients
Bead Soup used from Stephanie Sersich (Maine)
60mm painted brass disk pendant
21mm antiqued brass pewter S-hook clasp
cup of red, pink, orange, and/or green beads, various sizes

Beads used from Lori Anderson's Pantry
approximately 3 ft. (1m) 22-gauge antiqued brass wire
14 in. (36cm) 10mm wide hand-dyed dark pink silk ribbon
8 in. (20cm) antiqued brass double ring charm chain, 6mm round links
8 6mm 20-gauge antiqued brass jump rings
30–50 1½-in. (3.8cm) antiqued brass headpins
2 antiqued brass fold-over crimps

Utensils
- Chainnose pliers
- Flatnose pliers
- Crimping pliers
- Wire cutters
- Fray Check (optional)

The ultimate in bead soup— ladle out a heaping cup of hand-mixed beads and see what you can cook up! The ribbon used at the ends of the necklace helps reduce weight and gives a lovely pop of coordinating color. Experiment with your color patterns, and don't forget to add a variety of bead sizes!

Tip Seed beads make colorful alternatives to traditional metal spacers—and they're less expensive!

Recipe
Create the Centerpiece

1 Attach two brass jump rings through the hole in the pendant. Make a simple chain by connecting three sets of two jump rings. Attach the last set to the center of the chain. Make sure your pendant is hanging forward.

Tip To make sure the entire pendant shows, drop it down a bit from the bead dangles. Do this by making a simple jump ring chain (Step 1), by using a bail, or by making an extended wire wrap.

2 This recipe follows a bead pattern, but you don't have to be precise. Rather, start with larger beads and space them out evenly along the chain with either wrapped loops or a briolette wrap if the bead is top-drilled. For this chain, I used two dangles per link and placed one on each side of each link.

3 String a few beads on a headpin, adding two or three colors to one dangle. Make the first half of a wrapped loop, connect it to the chain link, and complete the wraps. Repeat Step 3 using different combinations of beads.

4 As the necklace begins to fill in with beads, hold it up periodically to check the balance and weight. If you add lots of large beads closely together, you'll end up with a denser necklace. If you add lots of small beads to the links, you'll end up with a more delicate necklace. Experiment to get the look you desire.

5 If you have gaps to fill in, string a few seed beads on a headpin and connect in the gaps on the chain with wrapped loops.

Finish the Necklace

6 Cut the silk ribbon into two 7-in. (18cm) pieces. Knot one end through an end chain link. Make a tight knot through the loop at the end of the ribbon. Repeat on the other end with the second ribbon. Trim the ribbon ends to match. Use Fray Check (if desired) on the ends of the cut ribbon.

7 Use fold-over crimps to finish the ribbon ends: Begin the fold with crimping pliers and complete by using flatnose pliers to press the ends in more tightly.

8 Open a 6mm jump ring and string it through the hole in the fold-over crimp and one side of the S-clasp. On the other end of the necklace, connect a 6mm jump ring to the fold-over crimp.

Tip As you accumulate bead soup on your work table, you may want to have a few bowls and pre-sort by color.

Zack's Watercress Soup

By Lori Anderson (Maryland)

Ingredients

Bead Soup used from Zachary Anderson (Maryland)

25mm pewter toggle

2 20mm pewter frog beads

Hank green seed beads, varying sizes and colors

Beads used from Lori Anderson's Pantry

6 in. (15cm) 18-gauge oxidized sterling silver wire

8 13mm hexagon rings

66 1½-in. (3.8cm) 20-gauge oxidized sterling silver headpins

17 6mm 20-gauge oxidized sterling silver jump rings

2 tablespoons of green, amber, and blue seed bead mix

Utensils
- *Roundnose pliers*
- *Chainnose pliers*
- *Flatnose pliers*

Tip When I work with a mix of similar colors, I load up all the headpins first. This way, I know if I've used too much of a particular color or not enough of another.

14

My son, Zachary, has an eye for color and a keen appreciation for the work that Mommy does. He decided to raid a bead store with me and pick out Bead Soup for me to work with, all on his own. When we were naming this piece, Zack wanted a focus on the frogs, but refused to believe people eat frog's legs. After sifting through piles of green and blue seed beads, and talking about ponds and things that grow near the water, we lit upon the name Watercress. So, no frogs were harmed in the making of this soup!

Recipe

1 Cut two 3-in. (7.6cm) pieces of 18-gauge sterling silver wire.

2 Make a wrapped loop with one wire through the loop of the toggle ring. String a seed bead, a frog bead, and a seed bead. Make another wrapped loop.

3 Make a wrapped loop with the remaining wire through the loop of the frog bead link from Step 1. String a seed bead, a frog bead, and a seed bead. Make a wrapped loop through a hexagon ring.

4 Use pairs of jump rings to connect seven more hexagon rings.

5 Connect a jump ring to the end of the toggle bar, and use a pair of jump rings to connect the bar to the end hexagon ring.

6 Make a dangle by stringing at least four seed beads of various colors and sizes on a headpin and making the first half of a wrapped loop. Make 66 dangles.

7 Connect six headpin dangles to each of the wrapped loops connecting the two frogs. Connect six headpin dangles to the wrapped loop connecting the toggle ring.

8 On the hexagon ring next to the frog bead, connect 12 headpin dangles, all on the same side of the ring. Stay between the frog's wrapped loop and the two jump rings.

9 Skip hexagon #2. On hexagon #3, connect 12 headpin dangles, all on the same side of the ring, staying between the jump rings. Work on the opposite side of the hexagon as you did in Step 8.

10 Skip hexagon #4. On hexagon #5, connect 12 headpin dangles, all on the same side of the ring, staying between the jump rings. Work on the same side of the hexagon as you did for hexagon #1.

11 Skip hexagon #6. On hexagon #7, connect 12 headpin dangles, all on the same side of the ring, staying between the jump rings. Work on the same side of the hexagon as you did for hexagon #3.

Summer Strawberry and Mint Soup

By Brandi Hussey (Texas)

Ingredients

Bead Soup used from Lori Anderson (Maryland)

24x25mm sterling silver focal ring
2 16x12mm prasiolite faceted nuggets
2 12mm large sterling silver Bali beads
70–90 5mm irradiated pink quartz faceted rondelles
Sterling silver toggle

Beads used from Brandi Hussey's Pantry

24 in. (61cm) sterling silver wire, 24-gauge
2 in. (5cm) 2mm rolo-style sterling silver chain, cut into 1-in. sections
70–90 1½-in. (3.8mm) sterling silver ball headpins
2 17x5mm dark pink freshwater stick pearls, side-drilled
8 10x10mm purple freshwater pearl flakes
4 4mm sterling silver daisy spacers
2 3mm 16-gauge jump rings

Utensils

- Roundnose pliers
- Chainnose pliers
- Bentnose pliers
- Wire cutters

This glamorous bracelet will lead to hundreds of design options. Try using your favorite focal bead instead of the sterling silver ring. Experiment with various color patterns. Try making it with different metals and beads! As you'll see in my companion piece made with coral and turquoise, you can make this gorgeous bracelet with virtually any bead under the sun.

Tip Depending on how big the chain links are, it may become increasingly difficult to wire the quartz onto the chain because the cluster of beads will get tighter and tighter. If this happens, just skip a link and continue on. The cluster of beads will be close enough that you shouldn't notice.

8 Finish the bracelet by adorning the focal ring. Make four pink quartz charms dangles and attach two to the wrapped loop of each prasiolite bead on the end closest to the focal ring.

Tip Use wrapped loops for the pink quartz dangles and the bead connections. With bracelets in particular, wrapped loops are more secure than plain loops.

Recipe
Bracelet Base

1 Cut eight 3-in. (7.6cm) pieces of 24-gauge sterling silver wire.

2 Make a wrapped loop at one end of a 3-in. piece of wire and connect one side of the focal ring. String a prasiolite nugget and make a wrapped loop above the bead. Repeat on the other end of the ring.

3 Make a wrapped loop at one end of a 3-in. piece of wire and connect the prasiolite nugget. String four purple freshwater pearl flakes and make a wrapped loop. Repeat on the other end.

4 Make a wrapped loop at one end of a 3-in. piece of wire and connect the pearl flakes. String a 4mm spacer, a 12mm Bali bead, and a 4mm spacer and make the first half of a wrapped loop. Repeat on the other end.

5 Connect a 1-in. (2.5cm) piece of chain to the open loop and complete the wraps. Repeat on the other end.

6 Make a wrapped loop at one end of a 3-in. piece of wire and connect the end chain link. String a freshwater stick pearl, make a wrapped loop, and connect the toggle ring. Repeat on the other end, but complete the wraps after the stick pearl and attach the toggle bar with two jump rings.

Dangles

7 String a pink quartz rondelle onto a headpin and attach it to a chain link with a wrapped loop. Continue making dangles and attaching two dangles to each chain link (one on each side).

Substitute Financial diet? This chunky coral and faux turquoise version follows the same directions but uses lighter-on-the-wallet materials.

—*by Lori*

Soup in the Butterfly Garden

By Lori Anderson (Maryland)

Ingredients

Bead Soup used from Rebecca Anderson (United Kingdom)

3.8cm purple dyed wood 2-hole button
3.8x2.5cm copper filigree butterfly
16 in. (41cm) 22-gauge purple craft wire
20mm white jade flower button
2 10mm pale pink Lucite bell flowers
2 10mm pale pink frosted Lucite bell flowers
2 6mm deep pink glass bell flowers
3 10-in. (25cm) pieces of ribbon
Assortment of flowers and 6mm beads
   from Bead Soup mix

Utensils

- Roundnose pliers
- Chainnose pliers
- Flatnose pliers
- Wire cutters
- Alligator clip or tape

Beads used from Lori Anderson's Pantry

24 in. (61cm) 7x5mm oval copper chain
5 in. (13cm) 20-gauge oxidized copper wire
7mm 18-gauge antiqued copper jump ring
2½ in. (6.4cm) 3x2mm antiqued copper chain
25 (approximately) 1½-in. (3.8cm) 21-gauge
   antiqued brass headpins

Imagine yourself enjoying a cup of soup in your flower garden, relaxing in the cool air of spring, when suddenly, a butterfly alights upon your soup bowl. The first sign of spring! This necklace challenged me in several ways. How should I make use of the lovely large purple button, the butterfly, the ribbon, the purple wire, AND the Lucite flowers? What to do? Follow along for this deceptively easy necklace.

Recipe

1 Cut two 8-in. (20cm) pieces of 22-gauge wire. Gently bend each piece of wire in half.

2 String an 8-in. piece of wire through both holes of the button so both ends exit the same side. Repeat with the remaining 8-in. wire in the opposite direction.

3 Using your fingers, tightly twist the two pieces of wire on the back side of the button so you end up with about 1½ in. (3.8cm) of wire. Make a wrapped loop with this now single piece of twisted wire and snip off the excess.

4 On the front of the button, string the filigree butterfly over the two remaining pieces of wire. Using your fingers, tightly twist the two pieces of wire on one side of the button so you end up with about 1½ in. of wire. Make a wrapped loop with this now single piece of twisted wire and snip off the excess.

5 String a 6mm glass flower and a 10mm Lucite flower onto a headpin. Make the first half of a wrapped loop, connect the loop on the filigree butterfly, and complete the wraps. Repeat.

6 Cut two 12-in. (30cm) pieces of 7x5mm oval copper chain. Open a copper jump ring. String an end link of a 7x5mm piece of chain, the wrapped loop on the back side of the button, the end of a 3x2mm piece of chain, and an end link of a 7x5mm piece of chain. Close the jump ring.

7 Position the chains so the smaller chain dangles behind and below the button focal. Using your Bead Soup mix, attach random beads to the chain with wrapped loops.

Tip I like to make the very bottom bead of the pendant chain the largest one. This lends balance to the necklace. When choosing beads, make sure your dangles don't overpower the look of your focal.

8 Make a briolette wrap through the shank of the 20mm white flower button. Open the last link of the large chain and string the wrapped loop. Close the chain's link. (If your chain has soldered links, use a jump ring to connect the flower clasp to the chain.)

9 Tie the ribbon together with a 1-in. (2.5cm) tail. Use tape or an alligator clip to secure the ends of the three pieces of ribbon and braid the ribbon tightly for about 5–6 in. (13–15cm). Knot the end.

10 String the braid through the end chain link and tie it into a loop, using the flower button as a gauge (make sure the button can slide through the ribbon ring). Tie, knot, and trim, leaving about ¾ in. (1.9cm) of ribbon on each side as decoration.

Bird Earrings

On a headpin, string a pink flower, a purple flower, a 3mm spacer, and a bird. Make a wrapped loop. Attach an earring wire. Make a second earring.

Butterfly Earrings

Make a butterfly dangle with a purple flower, a copper butterfly, and a corrugated copper round. String the butterfly component and four flower dangles on a jump ring. Attach an earring wire, making sure two flowers lie on each side of the earring wire. Make a second earring.

The Key to My Heart Is Good Cooking

By Lori Anderson (Maryland)

Ingredients

Bead Soup used from Cassie Donlen (Missouri)

37mm (total length) fine silver hook-and-eye clasp, Cassie Donlen
32x22mm lampworked heart on silver pendant, Cassie Donlen
3 15mm purple rectangle glass beads
3 15mm burgundy glass dagger beads, top-drilled
3 10mm cream and purple glass leaves, top-drilled
3 8mm sterling silver swirl beads
4 8mm mauve crystal pearls
5 8mm red Lucite rounds
  8mm dark brown Czech fire-polished round bead
5 6mm pale yellow glass pearls
4 6mm purple ceramic washers
9 3mm pewter daisy spacers

9 2mm copper rounds
21 in. (53cm) antiqued brass chain, 5x3mm links
12 in. (30cm) 22-gauge sterling silver wire
18 2-in. (5cm) 22-gauge steel headpins

Beads used from Lori Anderson's Pantry

3 ft. (.9m) 22-gauge oxidized sterling silver wire
18 in. (46cm) 20-gauge oxidized sterling silver wire
2¾ in. (7cm) skeleton key prepared with Renaissance Wax
4 7mm/16-gauge oxidized sterling silver jump rings
4 3mm/16-gauge oxidized sterling silver jump rings
9 3mm/16-gauge oxidized sterling silver jump rings

Utensils

- Roundnose pliers
- Chainnose pliers
- Flatnose pliers
- Wire cutters
- Renaissance Wax (optional)

It's often said that the way to a person's heart is through the stomach. Made with an incredible lampworked heart set on sterling silver and a vintage key, this design offers many options. Try dangling a gemstone from a copper branch, or position the key vertically. Mix up a bead soup of coordinating colors, and you have a winning combination.

Recipe
Pendant

1 Cut an 18-in. (46cm) piece of 22-gauge wire. Wrap the wire around one end of the key barrel in a back and forth "tangle." Use half the wire, make a 10mm loop below the key, and continue wrapping until the tangle is about 10mm wide. Repeat on the other end of the barrel.

2 With a 3mm jump ring, connect each loop on the heart pendant to a loop on the wire tangle.

Necklace

3 Cut a 3-in. (7.6cm) piece of 20-gauge wire and a five-link piece of brass chain. Make a wrapped-loop link with an amber rondelle, a spacer, a red round, a spacer, and a dark brown fire-polished bead. Connect one link end to the chain before completing the wraps.

4 Connect the other link end to the bow end of the key with a 7mm jump ring.

5 With 22-gauge headpins, make wire wrapped dangles:
　a. mauve crystal pearl
　b. spacer, red Lucite round, and spacer
　c. copper round, purple washer, and copper round
　d. yellow glass pearl
Using 2 in. (5 cm) of 22-gauge wire, briolette wrap:
　a. cream and purple leaf
　b. burgundy dagger bead

6 Open a 7mm jump ring. String the dangles and the fourth link of the chain. Close the jump ring.

7 With a 3mm jump ring, connect the fifth (end) link of chain and the ring of the clasp.

8 Cut a three-link piece of chain. Cut a 3-in. piece of 20-gauge wire. Make a wrapped-loop link with a purple rectangle, a silver swirl, and a yellow pearl. Connect the bead link to the three-link chain before completing the wraps.

9 Use a 3mm jump ring to connect the end of the link from Step 6 with the loop above the bit end of the key.

10 Repeat Step 3. Open a 7mm jump ring and string the dangles and the end (third) chain link. Cut a 5-link piece of chain. String the end link. Close the jump ring.

11 Cut a 2-in. piece of 20-gauge wire. Make a wrapped loop through the end chain link. String a purple rectangle, a spacer, and an amber rondelle. Make a wrapped loop.

12 Cut a 2-in. piece of 20-gauge wire. Make a wrapped-loop link with a brown fire-polished bead, a silver swirl, and a copper round.

13 Use a 3mm jump ring to connect the beaded links.

14 Cut a 2-in. piece of wire and make a wrapped loop. String a copper bead, a red Lucite round, and a crystal pearl. Make the first half of a wrapped loop.

15 Use a 3mm jump ring to connect the beaded link from Step 12 to the beaded link from Step 10.

16 Fold an 18-in. piece of chain in half. Connect the half-wrapped loop at the end of the bead link from Step 12 through both end links of chain. Complete the wraps.

17 Cut a 3-in. piece of 20-gauge wire. Make a wrapped loop through the middle link of the folded chain. String a copper bead, a silver swirl, a copper, an amber rondelle, a purple washer, and a copper. Make a wrapped loop.

18 Repeat Step 3. Open a 7mm jump ring, string the dangles and the wrapped loop at the end of the bead link from Step 15, and close the jump ring.

19 Cut a 3-in. piece of 20-gauge wire. Make a wrapped loop through the end 7mm jump ring. String a yellow pearl, a purple rectangle, and a copper bead. Make a wrapped loop.

20 With a 3mm jump ring, connect the end loop of the beaded link and the hook clasp.

CHAPTER TWO
THE FOCAL METHOD

Have you ever bought a focal bead and kept it on your work table for days (weeks!) because it's so beautiful, but you haven't thought of a way to do it justice? Wait no longer.

Another way to mix Bead Soup is to start with a focal. With this method, you can go in several directions with your imagination.

❍ Think about the style of the focal. If it's very ornate, a simpler necklace design might be the best choice. I've redone many a necklace from "trying-too-hard" syndrome. Don't be afraid to take things apart and start over if it doesn't sing to you.

❍ Think about layering your focal with filigree, adorning it with charms, or creating a tassel from the bottom of the bead. This works really well with simpler pendants.

The following designs show unique uses for pendants -- everything from the elegant and refined to the whimsical and unusual. You'll find ideas for virtually any focal you own!

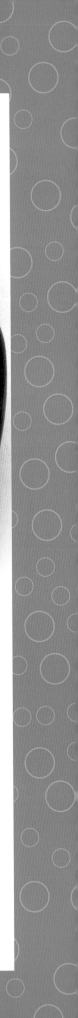

African Peanut Soup

By Lori Anderson (Maryland)

Ingredients

Bead Soup used from Lyn Foley (Texas)

3.8x2.5cm lampworked focal bead, Lyn Foley

4 4-in. (10cm) lampworked headpins with 10mm glass ends, Lyn Foley

20mm large-holed saucer bead

2 15mm batik beads

4 8mm dark brown wood washers

2 8mm black wood washers

Beads used from Lori Anderson's Pantry

2 23mm brass rings, Vintaj

3 12mm antiqued copper rings

4 6mm antiqued copper jump rings

6 3mm antiqued copper jump rings (closed)

2 2½-in. (6.4cm) antiqued copper headpins

5 ft. (1.5m) 3mm dark brown suede lacing

17 in. (43cm) 16-gauge antiqued copper wire

approximately 12 in. (30cm) dark brown DMC craft thread

9 in. (23cm) 10mm light tan doe skin lacing

Utensils

- Roundnose pliers (large and regular size)
- Chainnose pliers
- Flatnose pliers
- Heavy-duty wire cutters

- Regular wire cutters
- Hole punch pliers, ¼mm hole
- Sturdy needle
- Steel wool (optional)

This design is all about pattern. The focal had such a beautiful mix of colors, I decided to frame it with heavy-gauge wire. To keep the emphasis on the bead, I decided not to hammer or texture the wire. Choose leather for the length of the necklace or choose a copper chain for a different look. Experiment with various sizes of focal beads and wire and see what you can create!

This necklace shows that a bead can actually be a clasp! A large-hole bead can easily become just the component for an adjustable leather necklace, giving more flexibility in length.

Recipe
Make the Pendant

Tip For an oxidixed look, use Liver of Sulfer or JAX for copper to oxidize according to the manufacturer's instructions before beginning this project.

1 Using large roundnose pliers, make a wrapped loop at the end of the 16-gauge copper wire. String the 40x24mm lampworked bead.

2 Leaving a 10mm stem, closely pull the wire to the right of the focal bead with your fingers, keeping it snug to the bead. Wrap the wire around the stem twice and come back along the same side of the bead, leaving a 5mm space between the two wires.

Using your fingers, pull the wire in a gentle curve until it's about 15mm from the bottom of the focal bead. (See template for help.)

3 Use chainnose pliers to make a sharp bend in the wire at the 15mm center point where you left off in Step 2. Using your fingers again, gently curve the wire along the side of the bead, about 10mm from the edge of the focal bead. Finish by making a messy wrap around the stem and trim the end.

Tip Brush with steel wool on the high points to give depth to the wrap.

4 If necessary, use flatnose pliers to orient the wrapped loop perpendicular to the bead frame.

5 Attach two 6mm copper jump rings to the loop. Use two jump rings to attach the pendant to the 10mm closed copper ring.

Make the Dangles

6 String a lampworked headpin with a black washer and a copper washer. Make two. String a lamp-worked headpin with a brown washer and a copper washer. Make two.

7 Connect the dangles to the large copper ring with wrapped loops. Place one black washer headpin and one brown washer headpin on each side of the jump ring connection.

TEMPLATE

Make the Necklace

8 Make a lark's head knot through the large copper ring with the light tan doe skin. Be sure to keep the dangles below the knot.

Tip A soldered 10mm ring is best so you can give a good tug on the knot without worrying about the ring opening.

9 Trim the ends of the doe skin strips so they're even. Fold an end over a 23mm ring. Using the needle, make a mark in the center of the doe skin where your fold will hold the ring securely, but won't be too tight. Remove the ring.

10 Use a hand-held hole punch to punch a hole on each side of the needle mark. Fold the leather back over the gear ring, making a loop, and check the spacing. Keeping a grip on the doe skin so the punched holes are below the ring, gently punch back through the same holes. You'll have a total of four matching holes when you fold the leather over the gear rings.

11 Thread the needle with brown thread. Sew back and forth several times through the holes to secure the gear ring. Knot the sewing on the back and trim the thread. Repeat on the other end, marking your holes to match up with the first set.

12 Cut a 30-in. (76cm) piece of dark brown suede lacing. Make a lark's head knot through the 23mm gear ring. Repeat on the other end of the necklace. Trim the suede ends so they're even.

Make the Closure

13 On each end of the necklace, hold the two strands of suede lacing as one and string through the 20mm saucer bead in opposite directions.

Tip The laces should be snug in the bead hole in order to keep the necklace from lengthening on its own as you wear it, but not so tight the suede wears down.

14 Tie a pair of suede laces through a 10mm copper ring. Repeat with the remaining pair.

15 On a headpin, string a 3mm closed jump ring, a batik bead, a 3mm closed jump ring, a black washer, and a 3mm closed jump ring. Make a wrapped loop through the 10mm copper ring. Repeat on the other side.

To wear, pull both ends of the suede lacing so the beads move toward the big-hole bead. Put over your head, and pull the beaded ends equally to shorten the necklace to the desired length.

Chilled Blueberry Soup

By Lyn Foley (Texas)

Ingredients

Bead Soup used from Erin Prais-Hintz (Wisconsin)

2 40mm slabs of dyed blue banded agate
1¼ in. (3.2cm) sterling silver and resin clasp, Erin Prais-Hintz
2 25mm faceted teardrop opalite beads
16-in. (41cm) strand of 6mm dyed blue cultured pearls

Beads used from Lyn Foley's Pantry

2 14mm vintage silver metal beads
8 13mm vintage silver metal beads
11 13mm apatite rondelle beads
12mm sterling silver flower bead set with a moonstone
22 10mm dyed blue coin pearls
3-in. (7.6cm) 16-gauge handmade sterling silver headpin, Lyn Foley
3 ft. (.9m) beading wire
4 2x2mm sterling silver crimp tubes
13 size 11º blue seed beads

Utensils
- Roundnose pliers
- Crimping pliers
- Wire cutters
- Bead reamer (optional)

Blueberries! Just the word reminds me of hunting for blueberries in the wild tangle of bushes outside my grandmother's house. I'm quite sure I ate dozens more than ever hit my basket. This elegant necklace, which is made to be worn in two ways, is as versatile as my grandmother. Grandma was a simple lady who made her life as a tailor, and she would have worn the first strand every day. But there was a side of her that loved to dress up, and she also would have slipped the pendant extension over the single strand and danced the night away.

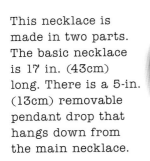

Recipe
Main Necklace

(Note: Before you begin, check to see that you can make two passes of wire through the pearls. If not, enlarge the holes with a bead reamer. Twist the reamer slowly and gently.)

1 Cut 20 in. (51cm) of beading wire. String and center a 40mm dyed blue agate bead.

2 On one end string a 6mm pearl, a coin pearl, * a 6mm pearl, a silver bead, a 6mm pearl, a coin pearl, an apatite bead, and a coin pearl. Repeat the pattern from the * three times.

3 String: 6mm pearl, silver bead, 6mm pearl, coin pearl, crimp, and a coin pearl. String seven seed beads. String the shank of the button and go back through the coin pearl and the crimp.

4 Snug the pearls, the crimp, and the seed beads tight into a circle. Crimp and cut the excess beading wire.

5 Repeat Step 2 on the other end.

6 String: 6mm pearl, silver bead, 6mm pearl, coin pearl, crimp, coin pearl, and the clasp hook. Go back through the coin pearl and crimp, check the length and fit of the necklace, and crimp.

The basic necklace is now complete and can be worn alone, if desired.

Removable Drop

7 On a 3-in. (7.6 cm) headpin, string the silver flower moonstone bead, a 40mm banded agate, and an apatite bead. Make a plain loop above the beads.

8 Cut 9 in. (23cm) of beading wire. Center the pendant on the wire. String a 6mm pearl, an opalite teardrop (small end first), a 6mm pearl, an apatite bead, a crimp bead, and 11 6mm pearls. Go back through the crimp bead and the apatite bead. Crimp the crimp bead. Repeat on the other end.

9 Slide each loop of the pendant drop over the clasp ends until the loops rest on either side of the central banded agate of the original necklace.

This necklace is made in two parts. The basic necklace is 17 in. (43cm) long. There is a 5-in. (13cm) removable pendant drop that hangs down from the main necklace.

Vegetable Garden Soup

By Heather Powers (Michigan)

Ingredients

Bead Soup used from Nan Emmett (Texas)

30mm ceramic bee pendant, Nan Emmett
4 20mm oval dark wood beads
4 15mm oval green howlite beads

4 12mm oval red jasper beads
4 10mm cream ceramic beads, Nan Emmett
4 8x4mm green howlite disks
brass flower clasp

Beads used from Heather Power's Pantry

4 14mm burgundy polymer clay disks, Heather Powers
12 4mm copper spacers
8 13mm links of brass oval chain
20 1½-in. (3.8cm) brass eyepins
4 7mm brass jump rings
10mm plain brass jump ring
10mm textured brass jump ring

Utensils
- *Roundnose pliers*
- *Chainnose pliers*
- *Wire cutters*

A bee in the garden means perfect vegetables! Before I began making jewelry for a living, I was an avid gardener, mapping out a blueprint for a vegetable and herb garden, building it from scratch, then planting it with every color and style of vegetable under the sun. This necklace, with its earthy colors and garden-appropriate bee pendant, reminds me of the amazing fruits of my labors. Experiment as I did with my garden—perhaps your garden is full of flowers! A pastel palette would be equally lovely in this simple, elegant style.

Recipe

1 Create a plain-loop link using the brass eye pins for the following:
   a. green howlite oval
   b. copper spacer, ceramic bead, copper spacer
   c. wood bead oval
   d. green howlite disk, copper spacer,
      polymer clay disk
   e. red jasper bead
Make four of each link.

2 Open the 10mm brass jump ring and link the pendant and the textured jump ring. Close the jump ring.

3 Make a connecting strand of: a, b, c, and d. Connect A to the textured jump ring.

4 Repeat Step 3 on the other side.

5 Open a brass chain link with chainnose pliers and use it as a jump ring to connect link d at the end of the strand and another link d.

6 Repeat Step 5 on the other side.

7 To the end of link d, attach a linked strand of c, b, a, e, e.

8 Attach three chain links to the last bead link e with a 7mm jump ring.

9 Repeat Steps 7 and 8 on the other side.

10 Attach the toggle bar to one end of the chain with a 7mm jump ring. Attach the toggle ring to the other end of the chain with a 7mm jump ring.

Substitute A similar bead can reap dramatically different results, as you can see by my bracelet made with a bee bead by Nan Emmett in a different colorway. The bracelet was made with a pewter toggle, polymer clay bead by Barbara Bechtel, a bee bead and rondelle in berry red by Nan Emmett, and a double strand of garnet and Peruvian pink opal. Experiment with your beads—fine gemstones can be mixed with more casual beads for a lovely effect!

—*by Lori*

Shiitake Mushroom Soup with Citron and Lavender Sea Salt

By Kerry Bogert (New York)

Ingredients

Bead Soup used from Lori Anderson (Maryland)

48x40mm Shibuichi pendant
15mm mosaic shell bead
2 20mm faceted citrine beads
21 6mm faceted Czech glass rondelles
16mm Shibuichi toggle clasp

Beads used from Kerry Bogert's Pantry

24 in. (61cm) 20-gauge bronze-colored copper wire
15 in. (38cm) brass rolo chain, cut into four 3¾-in. (9.5cm) pieces
2 5mm 21-gauge bronze jump rings

Utensils

- Roundnose pliers
- Chainnose pliers
- Wire cutters

Want a different look? Try designing a necklace with the pendant turned upside down!

Just like the gourmet ingredients in this soup recipe, the contrasting shades of deep lavender, lemony yellow, and earthy Shibuichi blend to create a design in perfect color harmony. Cloud-like swirls in the stunning pendant give the overall look a dreamy, vintage quality, yet the piece is appropriate for all occasions.

Recipe

1. Cut 20 2-in. (5cm) pieces of wire. Create two 10-bead chains of 6mm Czech glass beads by connecting with wrapped loops. Do not complete both final wraps on the last bead at one end of each chain. Do not complete one wrap on the other end of both chains.

2. Orient the pendant so the five loops are at the top. (The center loop will not be used.) Connect a beaded chain from Step 1 to the loop on each side of the center loop using the link with one open wrap. Complete the wraps.

3. Cut a 4-in. (10cm) piece of wire. Make a wrapped loop connecting the outside link on the pendant. String a citrine bead. Make a wrapped loop at the other end of the bead, attaching it to a 3¾ in. (9.5cm) piece of rolo chain. Repeat with the remaining outside loop on the pendant.

4. Link the end link of the beaded chain to the last link of the rolo chain by completing the wraps on the bottom loop. Repeat on the other end.

5. Attach the top link of the beaded chain to a 3¾-in. piece of rolo chain by completing the wraps. Repeat on the other end.

6. Open a bronze jump ring and connect the last link of a rolo chain to the bar end of the toggle clasp. Close the ring. On the other end of the necklace, connect the last link of the rolo chain to the ring end of the toggle clasp with a bronze jump ring.

7. Cut a 4-in. piece of wire. String a 6mm Czech glass bead on the wire and make a briolette wrap above the bead. Trim the excess short wire, leaving a long tail.

8. String the mosaic shell bead onto the long tail. Make a wrapped loop, and connect the dangle to the bottom loop of the pendant.

Waiter, There's a Ladybug in My Soup!

By Melissa Meman (Maryland)

Ingredients

Bead Soup used from Lori Anderson (Maryland)

45mm ceramic focal
20mm antiqued brass flower hook and eye clasp
6 10mm red Czech glass bell flower beads

Beads used from Melissa Meman's Pantry

38x25mm stamped brass component, Melissa Meman
16mm orange enameled bead, Melissa Meman
14mm blue enameled bead, Melissa Meman
2 11x6mm faceted Canadian jade rondelles
2 8x6mm faceted yellow calcite rondelles
4 8mm antiqued brass filigree beads
5 7mm light blue Czech glass flower beads

4 7mm dark blue Czech glass flower beads
2 7mm light green Czech glass flower beads
4 4mm Topaz Swarovski crystal bicones
2 4mm Indian Sapphire Swarovski crystal bicones
6 4mm brass bead caps, Melissa Meman
8 6mm brass bead caps, Melissa Meman
9 2-in. 22-gauge ball headpins, antiqued brass
1 ft. (30cm) 8mm link antiqued brass chain
10 in. (25cm) antiqued brass wire, 22-gauge, cut
　into 2-in. pieces
8 in. (20cm) 18-gauge wire, antiqued brass

Utensils

- Roundnose pliers
- Wire cutters
- Permanent marker (as mandrel)
- Steel bench block (optional)
- Chasing hammer (optional)

Ladybugs bring good luck—even if they end up paddling in your soup! So gently scoop the little lady out and send her on her way. This unique necklace has lots of design possibilities. Think about how it would look with red satin cording! When faced with a focal that has a very specific theme, let your own creativity shine.

Tip Try your own hand at stamping! Choose a brass blank and metal stamps from your local bead store, or take a class and discover an entirely new craft!

Recipe
Make the Pendant

1 Cut an 8-in. (20cm) piece of 18-gauge wire. Pass the wire through the hole in the pendant twice, leaving a 5-in. (13cm) tail. Wrap the short end around the tail and trim. With the tail, make a large loop around the marker perpendicular to the double wrap through the pendant. Make a wrapped loop, but instead of trimming, coil the end and flatten against the wrapped loop. Hammer lightly to add texture, if desired.

Tip For all red flowers, don't trim the wrapping wire—use roundnose pliers to make a small spiral and press it against the flower bead for added decoration.

Assemble the Necklace

2 Make dangles with beads on headpins, and wire wrap them directly to the pendant bail. On one side of the bail, make and connect:
   a. 7mm light blue flower
   b. 4mm topaz crystal and 10mm red flower
   c. 7mm dark blue flower
On the other side of the bail, make and connect:
   d. 7mm light blue flower
   e. 4mm Montana blue crystal and 10mm red flower
   f. 7mm dark blue flower

3 With a 2-in. (5cm) piece of 22-gauge wire, make a wrapped-loop link with a 4mm bead cap, a 8x6mm rondelle, and a bead cap. Connect one end to the bail above the dark blue flower, and the other end to the clasp hook.

4 With a 2-in. piece of 22-gauge wire, make a wrapped-loop link with an 8mm filigree bead. Connect one end to the bail above the light blue flower.

5 Cut a 2-in. piece of 22-gauge wire. Make a wrapped-loop link with a bead cap, the 16mm enameled bead, and a bead cap. Connect one end to the filigree link and leave the other end unwrapped.

6 Cut a piece of chain with three large links. Connect the enameled bead by completing the wraps. Make flower dangles with headpins and adorn the large chain links with two flower charms each:
   a. 7mm green flower; topaz crystal and 10mm red flower
   b. 4mm crystal and 10mm red flower; 7mm dark blue flower
   c. 7mm light blue flower; topaz crystal and 10mm red flower

7 Make and connect wrapped-loop links using 2-in. pieces of 22-gauge wire:
   a. 6mm bead cap, 14mm blue enameled bead, 6mm bead cap
   b. 4mm bead cap, 11x6mm jade rondelle, 4mm bead cap
   c. 8mm filigree bead, but do not complete the last wrapped loop

Tip Make the bail with a large jump ring instead of wire.

8 Connect the 8mm filigree bead to an end link of the 8mm chain. On the other end, add three flower charms strung on headpins:
   a. 7mm green flower charm
   b. 4mm topaz crystal and 10mm red flower charm
   c. 7mm dark blue flower charm

9 With a 2-in. piece of 22-gauge wire, make a wrapped-loop link with a 8mm filigree bead. Connect it to the end link of chain from Step 8.

10 On a 2-in. piece of wire, make a wrapped loop and connect it to the 8mm filigree bead. String a 4mm bead cap, an 8x6mm rondelle, and a 4mm bead cap and connect it with a wrapped loop to the top hole of the stamped component.

11 Connect a 2-in. piece of wire to the bottom of the stamped component with a wrapped loop. String a 6mm bead cap, an 11x6mm jade rondelle, and a bead cap. Make a wrapped loop.

12 Connect a 2-in. piece of wire to the jade link with a wrapped loop. String an 8mm filigree bead. Make a wrapped loop and connect it to the eye portion of the clasp.

Earrings

On a 2-in. piece of wire, make a wrapped loop through the hole in the ceramic disk, leaving a tail. Make a wrapped loop with the tail and connect an end link of chain. Connect two flowers with wrapped loops to one side of the chain link. Attach an earring wire. Make a second earring.

Portabella Mushroom and Caramelized Onion Soup

By Erin Prais-Hintz (Wisconsin)

Ingredients
Bead Soup used from Jennifer Cameron (Indiana)
42x20mm lampworked glass focal, Jennifer Cameron
2 13x15mm lampworked glass beads, Jennifer Cameron
15mm sterling silver hook clasp
16-in. strand of 4mm peacock cultured button pearls

Utensils
- Flatnose pliers
- Crimping pliers
- Heavy-duty wire cutters
- 000 steel wool or synthetic steel wool
- Alligator clips

Beads used from Erin Prais-Hintz's Pantry
3 22mm patterned pewter rings
15mm carved bone bead
4 10mm steel washers
8mm Black Diamond Swarovski crystal bicones
8 8mm antiqued silver oval jump rings
22 5mm Black Diamond Swarovski crystal bicones
74 5mm pewter daisy spacers
6 5mm steel washers
40 in. (1m) beading wire (.014mm or size that will go through pearls)
16 in. (41cm) 19-gauge dark annealed galvanized steel wire
tube matte topaz silver-lined beads
6 sterling silver crimp tubes
6 sterling silver crimp covers

Rich and full of flavor, this necklace is a feast for the eyes. Made with a mélange of textures and rich colors, this piece represents what can happen when you mix the humble (seed beads) with the amazing (handmade glass). Can you find beads in your bead drawer that are humble and amazing that can be mixed together in a new way?

Substitution To add a textural element, string three spacers onto each jump ring before closing. You can also use round jump rings if you can't find oval jump rings.

Recipe

1 Firmly rub steel wool or synthetic steel wool over the steel wire to completely clean off the dark coating.

Tip Steel will rust if it comes in contact with water. Do not use water when cleaning steel wire or let your jewelry become wet. You can also use 20-gauge oxidized sterling silver wire instead of steel wire.

2 Use the heavy-duty wire cutters to cut three 3-in. (7.6cm) and one 7-in. (18cm) pieces of 19-gauge wire.

Tip Never use regular wire cutters to cut steel wire—you'll ruin them in a heartbeat.

3 On a 3-in. piece of wire, make a wrapped-loop link. String: seed bead, spacer, 5mm steel washer, 10mm steel washer, seed bead, 13x15mm lampworked glass bead, 10mm steel washer, seed bead, 5mm washer, spacer, and seed bead. Make two links.

4 On a 3-in. piece of wire, make a wrapped loop. String: seed bead, spacer, 5mm steel washer, bone bead, 5mm steel washer, spacer, and seed bead. Complete the wrapped loop.

Tip To keep lampworked beads from wobbling on the beading wire, string small seed beads into the hole. Result—a stable bead on the wire!)

5 Using oval jump rings, connect the hook of the clasp, the lampworked bead link, the patterned pewter ring, the bone bead link, a patterned pewter ring, and a lampworked bead link.

6 Attach two oval jump rings to a patterned pewter ring. Close the jump rings.

7 Cut two 20-in. (51cm) pieces of beading wire. Center a wire on the end loop of the bead link from Step 5. Over both ends, string a crimp tube. Crimp, and cover with a crimp cover. Repeat with the second strand of beading wire.

8 Separate the four beading wire strands and string a random pattern of beads onto each, alternating between pearls, seed beads, spacers, and the 5mm crystal bicones. Secure each section at the end with an alligator clip, tape, or bead stopper.

9 Braid the four strands loosely and secure the ends: String a crimp tube, and a jump ring from Step 6. Go back through the crimp tube and tighten the wire. Crimp the crimp tube and cover with a crimp cover. Repeat with the other strands, crimping two strands to each jump ring.

10 On one end of the remaining 7 in. (18cm) piece of steel wire, create a spiral. String an 8mm crystal bicone and the 42x20mm lampworked focal bead. Make a wrapped loop connecting the link to the pewter ring from Step 9.

11 Use an oval jump ring to connect the clasp loop to the pewter ring from Step 9.

Stone Soup

By Malin de Koning (Sweden)

Ingredients

Bead Soup used from Lori Anderson (Maryland)

76mm river stone pendant with etched wildflower

22mm antiqued brass bird link

22mm Sleeping Beauty turquoise freeform slab

3 10mm faceted Sleeping Beauty turquoise briolettes

25 2mm antiqued brass cubes

22mm antiqued brass hook clasp

9 in. (23cm) brass chain, 20mm oval-3 8mm round
   link-20mm oval pattern

Beads used from Malin de Koning's Pantry

2 20x15mm pyrite ovals

8x6mm blue/green Czech faceted rondelle

7 8mm silver leaf agate puff squares

40 6x4mm Czech faceted rondelles in shades of blue, green,
   and yellow/beige

8 4mm antiqued brass heishi rings

2 4mm brass rounds

4 2mm brass rounds

4mm crimp beads

10mm brass jump ring

4 4mm oxidized brass crimp covers

16 in. (41cm) 20-gauge oxidized brass wire

12 in. (30cm) beading wire

3 1½-in. (1.3cm) pieces of 22-gauge oxidized brass wire

Utensils

- Roundnose pliers
- Chainnose pliers
- Flatnose pliers
- Crimping pliers
- Wire cutters

Most people have read the folk story *Stone Soup*. This necklace truly does start with a stone—a beautifully etched river stone! When I created this soup, I decided to pair the humble river rock with the most prized of all turquoise stones—Sleeping Beauty turquoise. Coordinating Czech glass and brass chain make this both a clever and beautiful piece of jewelry.

Recipe
Make the Pendant

1. Cut three 1½-in. (1.3cm) pieces of 22-gauge wire. Make briolette wraps above each faceted turquoise briolette. Connect each to the bottom ring of the bird link with a wrapped loop.

2. Cut a 1½-in. piece of 20-gauge wire and make a wrapped loop. String the 8x6mm blue/green Czech facetted rondelle. Complete the wrapped loop.

3. Open the 10mm brass jump ring and string it through the river stone pendant, the bird link, and one of the wrapped loops of the 8x6mm Czech bead. Close the ring.

Make the Chain Side of the Necklace

4 Create custom chain as in the sidebar below, or use the existing chain (cut into three 3-in. (7.6cm) segments).

5 Open and close a round end link of a 3-in. piece of chain, string it through the top wrapped loop of the pendant, and close the ring.

6 Cut a 2-in. (5cm) piece of 20-gauge wire and make a wrapped loop, connecting it through the end link of the piece of chain from Step 2. String a 6x8mm Czech glass rondelle and a pyrite oval. Make the first half of a wrapped loop, string a round end ring of a 3-in. piece of chain, and complete the wrapped loop.

7 Cut a 2-in. piece of 20-gauge wire and make a wrapped loop, stringing it through the end round link of the piece of chain before completing the wraps. String a pyrite oval. Make the first half of a wrapped loop, string a round end link of a 3-in. piece of chain, and complete the wrapped loop.

8 Open the end round link of the piece of chain, string the ring portion of the clasp, and close the ring.

Make the Beaded Side of the Necklace

(For the jump rings on this side of the necklace, use the leftover round 8mm rings from the deconstructed chain or two 8mm rings.)

9 Open a jump ring and string the top loop of the pendant. Close the ring.

10 Cut a 2½-in. (6.4cm) piece of 20-gauge brass wire. Make a wrapped loop, connecting it through the jump ring attached in Step 1. String the turquoise slab. Make a wrapped loop.

11 Make a beaded oval: string 25 2mm antique brass cubes on a 2½-in. piece of 20-gauge wire. String two crimp beads. Form the oval by hand and string the end of the wire back through both crimps. Crimp the crimp beads with crimping pliers. Cover the crimps with a 4mm oxidized brass crimp cover or two 2mm crimp covers.

12 Open a jump ring and connect the wrapped loop of the turquoise slab and the beaded oval. Close the jump ring.

13 On a 12-in. (30cm) piece of beading wire, string the beaded oval ring between two of the brass cubes. String a 4mm antiqued brass heishi ring, a crimp, and go back through both beads. Crimp the crimp, cover with a brass crimp cover.

14 String a 4mm brass round, a heishi ring, an 8mm jasper square, a heishi ring, a 2mm brass round, and a 4mm brass round, and a heishi ring.

15 Mix 39 of the 6x4mm green, blue, and yellow/beige Czech rondelles together and string them in random order on the beading wire.

16 String a heishi ring, a 2mm brass round, a 4mm brass round, a heishi ring, and six 8mm jasper squares.

17 String a heishi ring, a 2mm brass round, a crimp bead, and a heishi ring. String the beading wire through the loop of the hook part of the clasp and back through the heishi ring and the crimp. Crimp the crimp and cover with a crimp cover.

Option: Create a Unique Chain

1 The chain has an oval-three round ring-oval pattern. Deconstruct the chain by opening all of the links of the chain, setting them aside to make a new chain. You will need 40 round links and nine oval links to make the new chain sections.

2 Make a new piece of chain by linking 13 of the round links in a one-to-one sequence to make a 3-in. piece of round link chain.

3 Open and close an oval link and string it onto the first round link, skip three round links, and string the oval onto the fifth round link. This is the pattern.

4 Add another oval to the same round link, and repeat Step 3 until you create a 3-in. piece of chain of three oval links and 13 round links. Each piece of chain should start and finish with a round link. Make a total of three 3-in. pieces.

Cabin Fever Soup

By Jennifer Cameron (Indiana)

Ingredients
Bead Soup used from Melanie Brooks (Michigan)
35mm ceramic owl pendant, Melanie Brooks, (EarthenwoodStudio.com)
25mm ceramic toggle clasp, Melanie Brooks
2 10x14mm ivory ceramic beads, Melanie Brooks
2 8x12mm sage green ceramic beads, Melanie Brooks

Beads used from Jennifer Cameron's Pantry
2 20x12mm red and ivory shield-shaped lampworked beads,
   Jennifer Cameron, (JenCameronDesigns.etsy.com)
2 15x10mm red and ivory shield-shaped lampworked beads,
   Jennifer Cameron
3 10mm red-and-ivory nugget-shaped lampworked beads,
   Jennifer Cameron
8 3.5mm copper heishi spacers
2 ft. (61cm) 21-gauge brass wire
13 in. (33cm) 3mm brass cable chain
4 2-in. (5cm) brass headpins
15mm brass jump ring
21 4.75mm brass jump rings
7.25mm brass jump ring

Utensils
- *Roundnose pliers*
- *Chainnose pliers*
- *Flatnose pliers*
- *Wire cutters*

Sometimes the best escape is a cabin in the forest, especially in the winter. When I look at this bead mix, I imagine the toggle as the door of a tiny cottage in the woods, where a bird-watcher heads out at twilight to look for the most beautiful owls. The cream and sage ceramic beads remind me of button mushroom caps, and the lampworked beads are like lichen on rocks and trees. Of course, there's soup waiting in the cabin when the bird-watcher comes home.

Recipe

Note: Unless otherwise stated, jump ring size refers to 4.75mm.

1 Cut the 21-gauge wire into seven 3-in. (7.6cm) pieces. Make a wrapped-loop link with a 3-in. piece of wire and a 20x12mm red lampworked bead. Repeat to make seven lampworked bead links using the 20x12mm, 15x10mm, and 10mm beads.

2 On a headpin, string a copper heishi spacer, a ceramic bead, and a heishi spacer. Make a wrapped loop above the beads. Repeat with both colors of the remaining ceramic beads to make four bead dangles.

3 Using two jump rings, attach the owl pendant to the 15mm jump ring.

4 Cut a 3-in. piece of chain. Attach the owl pendant to the center link with two jump rings.

5 Attach an ivory ceramic bead dangle to each end link using jump rings. On each piece of chain, attach a sage green ceramic bead dangle between the ivory bead and the large jump ring.

6 Attach a larger red lampworked bead link to the end chain link (from Step 5) with a jump ring. Connect a smaller red lampworked bead link to the larger bead link with a jump ring. Repeat on the other end.

7 Cut a 1-in. piece of chain. Attach one end link of chain to the red lampworked bead link from Step 6 with a jump ring. Attach the remaining end link of chain to the toggle ring with two jump rings.

8 Cut a 1-in. piece of chain and attach one end link to a smaller red lampworked bead link (from Step 6) with a jump ring. Attach the remaining end link to one of the nugget lampworked bead links with a jump ring. Connect two lampworked nugget links with jump rings creating a chain of three nugget links.

9 Cut an 8-in. (20cm) piece of chain. Attach an end link to the lampworked nugget from Step 8. Attach a 7.25mm jump ring to the toggle bar portion of the clasp and connect it to the remaining end link of chain.

Summer Soup

By Cassie Donlen (Missouri)

Bead Soup used from Libby Leuchtman (Missouri)
57mm lampworked glass pod focal, Libby Leuchtman
6 12mm round aqua recycled glass beads
2 12mm Bali silver beads
8 11mm turquoise nuggets
6 10mm round pink Czech glass beads
7 8mm fluted olive Czech glass beads

2 8mm round peach recycled glass beads
5 5mm black and white striped glass beads
12mm sterling silver toggle clasp

Beads used from Cassie Donlen's Pantry
4 24mm pink big hole lampworked disk beads, Cassie Donlen
30 6º copper/brown seed beads
12 2-in. (5cm) sterling silver headpins
14 5mm jump rings
4 in. (10cm) of 5mm cable link chain
3 in. (7.6cm) of 12mm cable link chain
18 in. (46cm) of 14-gauge sterling silver wire
9 ft. (2.7m) of 26-gauge sterling silver wire

Utensils
- Roundnose pliers
- Chainnose pliers
- Wire cutters
- Liver of sulfer (optional)
- Fine steel wool or synthetic steel wool (optional)

Tip For an oxidized finish, place the clusters in a warm bath of liver of sulfer and polish gently with fine steel wool.

When I see this necklace, I think of summer—vibrant pink, a flower pod, the cool aqua of shaved ice, and swimming pools. Feminine and flirty, it's a perfect summer-party adornment. Although this necklace does incorporate wirework, it's as simple as making a loop, bending a piece of wire in half, and wrapping the wire a few times around another. Deceptively simple, you'll wow your guests when you show up at the cook-out wearing this stunner!

Recipe
Necklace

1 Make a set of six dangles by stringing a seed bead and one of the following accent beads on a headpin: peach glass bead, pink glass bead, Bali silver bead, turquoise nugget, black-and-white glass bead, fluted olive bead. On each headpin, make a wrapped loop above the beads large enough to slide over the 5mm link chain. Repeat to make a second set.

2 Cut a 1¾-in. (4.4cm) piece of 5mm link chain. Center the focal bead on the chain. String six dangles on each end.

3 Cut a 3-in. (7.6cm) piece of 14-gauge wire. Make a plain loop on one end. String a 12mm aqua bead. Make a plain loop in the opposite direction at the other end. Bend the wire into an elongated S-shape. Make six beaded S-links.

4 Cut a 6-in. (15cm) piece of 26-gauge wire. String and center a seed bead. Fold the wire in half. String an accent bead over both wire ends. Repeat to make 18 beaded wires using the remaining pink, peach, olive, and black-and-white beads.

5 Group the beaded wires made in Step 4 into six clusters of three beads each. Hold a cluster in one hand and the wires in your other hand. Twist the wires into one thick strand. Make six cluster sets.

6 Wrap the wires of a cluster made in Step 5 around the end of an S-link about four times. Trim the excess wire and flatten the ends with chainnose pliers.

7 With a jump ring, attach a wired S-link to an end link of chain from Step 2. Cut a 4-link piece of 5mm link chain and attach it to the other end of the S-link. String a lampworked disk on the chain, and attach the end link to a new S-link with a jump ring. Repeat for a total of three wired S-links and two lampworked disks on each side.

8 Cut a 1½-in. (3.8cm) piece of 12mm link chain. Use jump rings to attach an end link to one end of an S-link and the other end link to the toggle bar. Repeat on the other end, substituting the toggle ring.

Earrings

1 Make two S-links as in Step 3 for the necklace. Make two beaded clusters as in Steps 4 and 5 of the necklace.

2 Attach a bead cluster to each S-link as in Step 6 of the necklace.

3 String a lampworked disk onto a 1-in. (2.5cm) piece of chain. Use a jump ring to connect both ends of chain to the loop on a bead cluster. Repeat for the other earring.

4 Attach an earring wire to each S-link.

Bird's Nest Soup

Ingredients

Bead Soup used from Lori Anderson (Maryland)
60x40mm bronze bird focal
35mm acrylic yellow polka dot lentil bead
20mm red Czech glass disk
3 10mm copper wavy disks
2-in. (5cm) vintage brass hook-and-eye clasp

Beads used from Sharon Palac's Pantry
30x15mm copper leaf, Sharon Palac
20mm copper wire bird's nest with pearl egg, Sharon Palac
3 10x14mm Owyhee jasper beads
8 7x4mm Picasso gold Czech glass leaf beads, top-drilled
13 6mm/18-gauge copper jump rings
27 in. (69cm) antiqued copper chain
26 in. (66cm) 22-gauge copper wire

Utensils
- Roundnose pliers
- Chainnose pliers
- Flatnose pliers
- Wire cutters
- Liver of sulfur (optional)

This necklace is as unique as the soup it's named for. The bold bird focal creates a challenge for the designer—how to make a piece that focuses on the bird, but as a whole is interesting and creative? Using a range of beads in complementary colors and adding whimsical charms to the focal makes this necklace stand out from the flock.

Recipe
Necklace Side One

1 Cut a 3-in. (7.6cm) piece of wire. Make a wrapped-loop link with an Owyhee bead. Open a jump ring and connect the right side top loop of the bird focal and the bead link.

2 Cut 3-in. piece of wire. Make the first half of a wrapped loop at one end and connect the bead link from Step 1. Complete the wraps. String an Owyhee bead and make a wrapped loop.

3 Cut 3-in. piece of wire. Make the first half of a wrapped loop at one end and connect the bead link from Step 2. String an Owyhee bead. Make the first half of a wrapped loop and connect the hook half of the clasp. Complete the wraps.

Necklace Side Two

4 Connect a 6mm jump ring to the top loop of the pendant. Connect three additional jump rings to make a four-ring strand.

5 Cut a 3-in. piece of wire. Make a wrapped loop through the last ring in the four-jump ring length. String two glass leaves and the 20mm glass disk. Make a wrapped loop above the beads.

6 Cut a 4-in. (10cm) piece of wire and make a wrapped loop at one end. String three 10mm copper wavy disks, two glass leaves, and the 35mm acrylic lentil. Make a wrapped loop above the beads. Use a 6mm jump ring to connect the end link from Step 5 with the bottom loop on the acrylic lentil unit.

7 Fold the chain into thirds for a three-strand, 9-in. (23cm) piece. Use a 6mm jump ring to connect the loop at the end of the acrylic bead unit and three of the chain's links.

8 Open a 6mm jump ring. At the other end of the chain, string the end link of one chain and the center link of the folded section. Close the ring. Attach a 6mm jump ring to the jump ring on the chain. Use a jump ring to connect the links and the smaller ring of the eye of the clasp.

9 Cut three 2-in. (5cm) pieces of wire. Make a briolette wrap above each of three glass leaves, and then make a wrapped loop above the wraps.

10 Open a 6mm jump ring, and pick up the leaves and the jump ring connecting the three-jump ring chain to the antiqued chain. Close the jump ring.

Embellish the Pendant

11 Connect the bird's nest charm to the bottom loop of the pendant with a 6mm jump ring.

12 Cut a 2-in. piece of wire. Make a briolette wrap above a glass leaf, and a wrapped loop above the wraps.

13 Use a 6mm jump ring to connect the handmade copper leaf and the glass leaf to the bottom loop of the pendant.

Earrings

1 String a wire bead on a headpin through an open space and make a wrapped loop.

Tip If your headpin slides completely through the wire bead, string a 4mm copper bead first, and then the wire bead.

2 Make the first half of a wrapped loop at the end of a 4-in. piece of copper wire. Connect the wire bead, and complete the wraps.

3 String the red Czech glass disk and make a wrapped loop. Connect the dangle to the earring wire. Make a second earring.

Bird's Nest Soup Earrings

Ingredients

- 2 20mm red Czech glass disk beads
- 2 25mm scribble wire beads
- 8 in. (20cm) 22-gauge copper wire cut into 2 4-in (10 cm) pieces
- 2 2-in. (5cm) 22-gauge copper headpins
- 2 4mm round copper beads (optional)
- 2 copper earring wires

Handmade Soup Bowls

By Cindy Wimmer (Virginia)

Bead Soup used from Kerry Bogert (New York)
32mm lampworked focal, Kerry Bogert
2 25mm flat leather disk beads, teal
10 8mm Czech faceted rondelle beads, Picasso blue
11 8mm Czech glass round beads, teal
10 6mm brass ridged rounds
30 in. (76cm) hand-dyed silk string, sage green
30 in. (76cm) hand-dyed 10mm silk ribbon, teal
14mm enameled toggle clasp, teal

Beads used from Cindy Wimmer's Pantry
2 5mm oxidized brass jump rings
8 6mm oxidized brass jump rings
31 2mm oxidized brass rounds
31 2-in. (5cm) oxidized brass headpins
12 in. (30cm) 24-gauge oxidized brass wire
17 in. (43cm) 18-gauge oxidized brass wire

Utensils
- Roundnose pliers
- Chainnose pliers
- Wire cutters
- Fray Check (optional)

I don't know about you, but I'm a huge fan of handmade soup bowls. This necklace contains beads that remind me of the best pottery and glass dishes I've purchased. The toggle, positioned right above the handmade glass focal, is adorned with bead dangles, but you could just as easily leave the dangles off and showcase a special toggle—just like you might display your favorite bowls in the china cabinet.

Recipe

1. On a headpin, string a 2mm round and a 6mm brass ridged bead. Make a wrapped loop. Make 10 dangles.

2. On a headpin, string a 2mm brasss round and an 8mm rondelle. Make a wrapped loop. Make 10 rondelle dangles.

3. On a headpin, string a 2mm round and an 8mm round. Make a wrapped loop. Make 11 round bead dangles.

4. Cut a 5½-in. (14cm) piece of 18-gauge wire. Make a plain loop at one end. String the 32mm lampworked bead. Make the first half of a wrapped loop ¼ in. (6mm) from the top of the lampworked bead. String the wire around the enameled toggle ring, and, in random order, string two brass ridged dangles, two rondelle dangles, and three round bead dangles. Complete the wrapped loop with 5–6 wraps, creating a long stem.

Tip Making a long stem keeps the bead dangles from covering part of the focal bead. You can also accomplish this look by adding jump rings to the wrapped loop and then adding the bead dangles.

5 Cut a 5½-in. piece of 18-gauge wire. Make a wrapped loop large enough for the ribbons to be strung through later. String a flat leather disk bead and make the first half of a wrapped loop. Connect the link to the small hole in the enameled toggle ring and complete the wraps.

6 Cut a 5½-in. piece of 18-gauge wire. Make a wrapped loop large enough for the ribbons to be strung through later. String a flat leather disk bead and make a wrapped loop.

7 Attach a 5mm jump ring to the toggle bar. Open a 5mm jump ring and connect the leather disk link from Step 6 to the to jump ring on the toggle bar.

8 String the ends of the sage cording and teal ribbon through the wrapped loop of a flat leather disk bead. Leave a ½-in. (1.3cm) tail. Use a 6-in. (15cm) piece of 24-gauge wire and wrap the wire around the folded ribbons several times to secure. Tuck in the wire ends.

9 String a 6mm jump ring over the sage silk cording. Make an overhand knot with both ribbons ¾ in. (1.9cm) from the end, securing the jump ring in the knot. String a jump ring on the teal ribbon. Make an overhand knot with both ribbons 2 in. (5cm) from the previous knot, securing the jump ring in the knot and making sure the knot is tied in the same direction as the previous knot. Repeat for a total of eight knots approximately 2 in. apart.

10 Carefully open a jump ring you just knotted and attach one brass ridged dangle, one round bead dangle, and one rondelle dangle. Close the jump ring. Repeat for all the jump rings.

11 String the ends of the cording and ribbon through the wrapped loop of the remaining round leather disk link. Trim the ribbons to match and secure with a 6-in. piece of 24-gauge wire as in Step 8. If desired, apply Fray Check to the cut ends of the ribbons.

CHAPTER THREE
THE COLOR PALETTE METHOD

COLOR! My favorite part of beading is the sheer wealth of colors available. Bead Soup can be mixed using color palette books that graphic designers use, paint chip design leaflets from hardware stores, or color pattern websites such as colourlovers.com. Start pulling beads from your stash, and add them to a bowl until you have an assortment that is both the right color and the right texture. Decide if you want a mix of large and small beads, or a profusion of same-sized beads.

A color wheel is a terrific design tool. Colors directly across from each other are complementary colors and look well together. Analogous colors are next to each other or close together on the color wheel, creating a subtler look. But monochromatic doesn't have to mean just ONE color! For instance, if you want to make a blue bracelet, consider using various shades of blue together to create a pleasing effect.

For a more whimsical, daring look, draw a triangle on the wheel—such as purple, green, and orange, and use those colors (or shades of those colors) for excitement. How bright or intense each color is or how *much* of a color you use in your palette can drastically change the look as well.

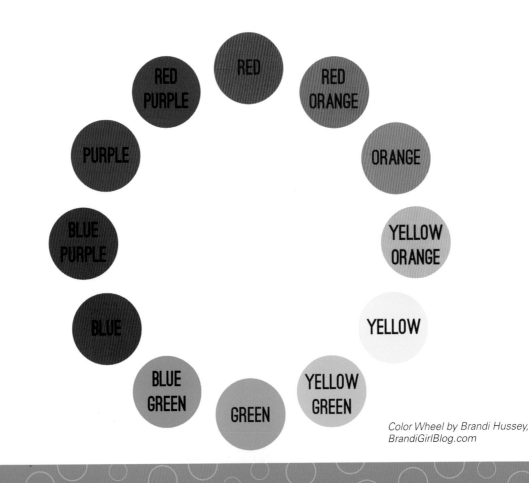

Color Wheel by Brandi Hussey, BrandiGirlBlog.com

Blue Crab Soup with Chilies

By Shannon LeVart (Missouri)

Ingredients
Bead Soup used from Christine Damm (Vermont)

45mm polymer clay donut focal, Christine Damm
4 30x20mm red, teal, and white polymer clay tube beads, Christine Damm
50mm beaded brass hook and eye clasp, Christine Damm
2 20x15mm teal turtle agate rectangle beads
18 15mm gray recycled African glass beads
4 15mm gold Greek ceramic tubes
4 12mm gold Greek ceramic rounds
4 8mm corrugated brass saucers
6 6mm teal blue Czech glass rounds
25 4mm corrugated brass rounds
16-in. (41cm) strand of 6mm amazonite chips
16-in. strand of 6mm African opal chips

Beads used from Shannon LeVart's Pantry
Dark red waxed linen

Utensils
- Roundnose pliers
- Chainnose pliers
- Wire cutters
- Scissors
- Jewelers cement

This stunning neckpiece mixes two of my favorite foods—crabs and chilies—into one amazing soup, and better yet, you're allowed to mix up your own flavors in each of the four strands. Want things hotter? Add more red chilies. Less spicy? Add the cooling waters of the Chesapeake. And the optional chain waterfall is a surprisingly simple way to create a beautiful addition.

Recipe
Necklace

1 To create a 20-in. (51cm) necklace, cut four 30-in. (76cm) strands of waxed linen.

2 Center the polymer clay donut focal on two strands of linen. Re-position the strands so two strands are on the front of the donut and two strands are at the back. Gather the sets of strands from the front and the back and tie an overhand knot with all four strands tight against the outer edge of the donut. Repeat on the other side of the donut. You should now have a knot on the top right edge of the donut with four strands of waxed linen and a knot on the top left edge with four strands of linen.

3 Mix together all the listed beads for the necklace and begin stringing one strand of waxed linen with the bead soup mix. String randomly, mixing up colors, textures, and shapes until you have a 9-in. (23cm) strand of beads that ends with a bead with a small hole. Knot the linen against the last small-holed bead and begin stringing the remaining strands of linen randomly in the same way.

Tip If you aren't sure you like your mix and are afraid to knot it until all your strands are completed, clip the waxed linen with an alligator clip and begin working on other strands. This prevents all your beadwork from sliding off the strands you just completed!

4 Once all eight strands have been strung and knotted with the tasty mix of beads, gather four strands on one side of the necklace and slide on the toggle clasp. Tie a knot as tight to the end beads of all four strands as you can. Place a drop of jewelers cement on the knot. Repeat on the other end, substituting the clasp loop.

5 Let the jewelers cement cure to the point where it can be touched (approximately 20 minutes), wrap four strands of the linen tail around the cemented knot, and gently roll the knotted Irish linen between your fingers. This movement bonds the waxed linen fibers to the cement glue and makes a stronger finish. Repeat on the other end.

Waterfall Embellishment

For an additional challenge and an even more interesting design, try adding the waterfall embellishment!

Ingredients
Bead Soup used from Christine Damm (Vermont)
15mm red dyed sea bamboo stick bead
14mm verdigris patina shell charm
Leftover amazonite and African opal chips from necklace
12 in. (30cm) 22-gauge antiqued brass wire
10 1–2-in. (2.5–5cm) sections antiqued bronze 3mm cable chain

Beads used from Shannon LeVart's Pantry
Dark red waxed linen cord

Recipe
Waterfall

1. Cut a 3-in. (7cm) piece of wire. Bend it gently in half.

2. String 10 chain pieces onto the bent wire in random order. Slide the wire ends through the center hole of the donut until you can't see the wire and the chain flows.

3. Start a wire spiral with chainnose pliers, with the wire protruding from the back of the donut. Switch to the chainnose pliers to finish the wire swirl and press down firmly against the back of the donut to hold the chain in place in the front of the donut.

4. Add beads and charms to the ends of a few strands of chain, including the shell charm and bamboo stick bead, wire-wrapping each bead and charm into place with the remaining antiqued brass wire.

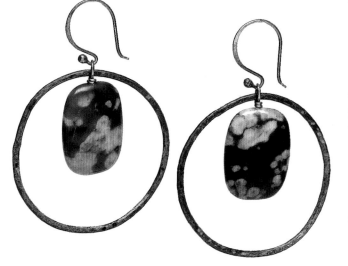

Recipe
Earrings

1. String a rectangle bead onto a headpin. Make a wrapped loop over the patinated copper hoop.

2. Gently open the loop of the earring wire and slide the wrapped loop of the rectangle bead over it. Close the earring wire. Make a second earring.

Earrings

Ingredients
2 20x15mm teal turtle agate rectangle beads
2 40mm patinated copper hoops
2 2½ in. (6cm) oxidized sterling silver headpins
2 oxidized sterling silver ear wires

Ginger Peach Soup

By Lori Anderson (Maryland)

Ingredients

Bead Soup used from Brandi Hussey (Texas)

30x20mm peach aventurine faceted rectangle
2 25x20mm chrysoprase slabs
2 20mm citrine-colored glass faceted nuggets
4 10mm dark amethyst faceted briolettes
8mm light purple amethyst faceted round
15 10mm sterling silver flower bead caps
20mm sterling silver toggle

Beads used from Lori Anderson's Pantry

5 14mm peach lampworked beads
8 6mm dark amethyst faceted rounds
12 4mm dark amethyst faceted rondelles
36 3mm chrysoprase faceted rondelles
3-in. (7.6cm) sterling silver Bali bead tassel
36 1½-in. (3.8cm) 26-gauge sterling silver headpins
16 7mm 16-gauge sterling silver jump rings
3 4½mm 16-gauge sterling silver jump ring (for toggle bar)
2 4.5mm 16-gauge sterling silver jump rings (for pendant)
3mm 16-gauge sterling silver jump rings (for pendant)
34 in. (86cm) sterling silver 3x4mm link chain
30½ in. (77.5cm) 20-gauge sterling silver wire
3½ in. (8.9cm) 16-gauge sterling silver wire
4½ in. (11.4cm) 26-gauge sterling silver wire (for briolettes)

Utensils
- Chainnose pliers
- Flatnose pliers
- Wire cutters
- Fine-point chainnose pliers (optional)

Ginger Peach Soup is a special soup for the summer—cool and exotic. This necklace is deceptively simple to make and as delectable as its namesake. It will take a little time and some meticulous wrapping to make all the little dangles, but once each beaded component is made first, then linked together with jump rings, the necklace can be put together in short order.

Recipe

Make the Pendant

1. On a 1½-in. (3.8cm) 26-gauge headpin, string a 3mm chrysoprase rondelle. Make a wrapped loop above the bead. Make a total of 36 dangles (12 for the pendant and 24 for the necklace).

2. On a 1½-in. 26-gauge headpin, string a 4mm dark amethyst rondelle. Make a wrapped loop above the bead. Make a total of 12 dangles for the pendant.

3. Make a wrapped loop at one end of the 16-gauge wire. String a light amethyst round, a silver flower bead cap (curve cupping the amethyst bead), and a peach aventurine rectangle. Make the first half of a large wrapped loop.

4. String the chrysoprase dangles on the open loop of Step 3. Using fine-point chainnose pliers, finish the wrapped loop.

Tip Fine-point chainnose pliers are very helpful when filling up a loop with many tiny dangles, as there is very little room to hold the wire to finish the wrapped loop. However, in order to make a full cluster of dangles, the loop needs to be as small as the dangles will allow.

5. Open a 4.5mm 16-gauge jump ring. String six amethyst dangles, the loop of the pendant holding the chrysoprase dangles (doing your best to keep half the chrysoprase dangles on either side), and six amethyst dangles. Close the jump ring.

6. Open a 3mm 16-gauge jump ring. String the jump ring with the amethyst dangles (doing your best to keep half the amethyst dangles on either side) and the Bali tassel. Close the jump ring.

7. Connect the pendant and the loop of the toggle ring with a 4.5mm 16-gauge jump ring.

Make the Bead Links

8. Make a wrapped loop at one end of the 4½-in. (11.4cm) piece of 26-gauge wire. String four amethyst briolettes, orienting them as shown in the photo. Finish with another wrapped loop.

NOTE: The following bead sections are all made with 20-gauge wire.

9. With a 3-in. (7.6mm) piece of wire, make a wrapped-loop link with a chyrsoprase slab. Repeat to make two chrysoprase links.

10 Cut a 2½-in. piece of wire and make a wrapped loop link with a flower bead cap (curve down), a lampworked bead, a flower bead cap (curve up), and a 6mm dark amethyst bead. Repeat to make a total of three lampwork and amethyst links.

11 Cut a 2½-in. piece of wire and make a wrapped-loop link with a citrine-colored glass nugget. Make a total of two citrine glass links.

12 Cut a 2½-in. piece of wire and make a wrapped-loop link with a flower bead cap (curve down), a lampworked bead, and a flower bead cap (curve up). Make a total of two of lampwork links.

13 Cut a 2½-in. piece of wire and make a wrapped-loop link with a 6mm dark amethyst round, a flower bead cap (curve down), 12 chrysoprase dangles reserved from Step 1, a flower bead cap (curve down), and a 6mm dark amethyst round. As you make the second wrapped loop, gently wrap the tail so the dangles create a dense cluster. Make a total of two links.

14 Cut a 1½-in. piece of wire. Make a wrapped loop and string a 6mm dark amethyst round. Make a wrapped loop.

Connect the bead links

15 Connect a 4.5mm 16-gauge jump ring to the loop on the toggle clasp. Connect a 4.5mm 16-gauge jump ring to this ring making a two-link chain.

16 Use 7mm 16-gauge jump rings to connect (in the following order) Strand A: toggle, chrysoprase cluster link, lampworked/amethyst section.

17 Use 7mm 16-gauge jump rings to connect (in the following order) Strand B: chrysoprase slab, lampworked/amethyst link, plain lampworked link.

18 Use 7 mm 16-gauge jump rings to connect (in the following order) Strand C: amethyst round link, plain lampworked link, chrysoprase cluster link, citrine nugget, citrine nugget, lampworked/amethyst link, chrysoprase slab, amethyst briolette link.

19 Cut a 26-in. piece of sterling silver chain. Fold the chain into four equal strands. String an open 7mm jump ring through the four end links of the chain and the wrapped loop of the single amethyst bead at the end of Strand C. Close the jump ring.

20 Open a 7mm jump ring and string the four links at the other end of the chain and a plain lampworked section at the end of Strand B. Close the jump ring.

21 Gather the remaining 8 in. (20cm) of chain into four equal strands. String an open 7mm jump ring through the end links of the chain and the wrapped loop of the chrysoprase slab section from Strand B. Open another jump ring and string it through the four links at the other end of the chain and an amethyst/lampworked bead section at the end of Strand A. Close the jump ring.

22 Open a 7mm jump ring and connect the wrapped loop of the amethyst briolette link from Strand C to the loop portion of the clasp.

By Nan Emmet (Texas)

Twice Cooked, Twice as Good

Ingredients
Bead Soup used from Barbara Bechtel (Florida)
30x40mm polymer clay pendant, Barbara Bechtel
15mm purple faceted polymer bead, Barbara Bechtel
15mm brass toggle

Beads used from Nan Emmet's Pantry
59mm Vintaj brass filigree (FL390)
57mm Vintaj brass prong filigree (FL370)
20mm clear faceted glass nugget
16mm clear faceted glass nugget
4 10mm copper luster Czech fire-polished rounds
3 10mm blue Czech fire-polished rounds
9x6mm blue Picasso Czech fire-polished rondelle

40 6mm blue Czech fire-polished rounds
6 4mm blue Czech fire-polished rounds
2 12mm brass filigree bead caps
10 7mm brass bead caps
11 6mm brass jump rings
4 brass crimp tubes
4 brass crimp covers
2 9mm textured brass jump rings
7 2-in. (5cm) brass headpins
25 in. (6.4cm) brass wire, 20-gauge
15 in. (38cm) beading wire

Utensils
- Roundnose pliers
- Chainnose pliers
- Flatnose pliers
- Wire cutters
- Crimping pliers

In the online Bead Soup Blog Party, the rules state that the recipient is required to use only the focal and the clasp. Using the accompanying accent beads is optional, and the object is to include beads from your own stash and push your design potential in new directions. Often a designer is challenged because the beads she receives are completely unlike what she's used to working with. In most of the projects in this book, the majority of the soup beads have been incorporated into the finished designs. In this innovative how-to, Nan Emmett chooses only one accent bead to accompany the focal and toggle. As a special twist to this Bead Soup, Nan returned the beads she didn't use, and Barbara generously gave me the same pendant. Nan and I wanted to see what I could do with the remaining beads, and at the same time, show you how differently two people can envision a design from similar ingredients.

Recipe
Make the Pendant

1 Place the pendant on the front of the 57mm prong filigree and gently bend the prongs with chainnose pliers to wrap around the pendant's edges. Center the wrapped pendant on the 59mm filigree component.

2 Turn the two pieces facedown and working from the back, attach each side of the wrapped pendant to the 59mm filigree with 6mm jump rings, one at the top, bottom, and each side of the 57mm filigree.

3 Turn the pendant back over, and attach a textured 9mm jump ring to the top of the pendant. Attach a textured 9mm jump ring to the existing jump ring.

4 On a balled headpin, string a 7mm brass bead cap, a 16mm clear glass nugget, and a brass bead cap. Make a wrapped loop above the beads. Attach the dangle to the bottom of pendant with a 6mm jump ring.

Side One

5 Cut four 3-in. (7.6cm) pieces of brass wire. Make a plain loop at the end of a wire and connect it the top textured ring of the pendant. String a 7mm brass bead cap, a 10mm blue Czech glass bead, and a 7mm brass bead cap on the wire. Make a plain loop.

6 On a 3-in. wire, make a plain loop and connect it to the end loop of the previous link. String a 7mm brass bead cap, a 10mm blue Czech glass bead, and a 7mm brass bead cap on the wire. Make a plain loop. Repeat once for a total of three linked brass capped blue beads.

7 On a 3-in. wire, make a plain loop and connect the end loop of the brass capped blue bead link. String a 7mm brass bead cap, a 20mm clear glass nugget, and a brass bead cap. Make a plain loop. Be sure the loop is tightly closed without a gap.

8 Cut a 7½-in. (19.1cm) piece of beading wire. String a crimp, the plain loop of the clear glass link, and back through the crimp. Crimp the crimp bead and cover with an antiqued brass crimp cover.

9 String a 4mm light blue bead on a headpin and make a wrapped loop. Make three dangles. Open a jump ring, string the three dangles, and close the jump ring around the beading wire. The jump ring will slide down over the crimp cover as you start beading.

10 String 20 6mm blue Czech glass beads on the beading wire. String a crimp bead and a jump ring. Go back through the crimp. Crimp the crimp bead and cover with a antiqued brass crimp cover.

Tip When stringing a long length of the same sized beads, be sure to crimp a little looser than normal. A tight crimp will cause a tight, inflexible necklace. You can also add 2mm beads or tiny spacers periodically between the beads to help break up the stiffness.

Substitute

I took an entirely different direction from Nan's amazing necklace. I never would have thought of filigree! In my piece, I used the rest of the beads in the Bead Soup, including another pendant from Barbara Bechtel. I wanted the bird to sit in a tree—hence the wood, wrapped in wire. And birds remind me of flowers, so the flower fringe chain worked for me. Neither necklace is better than the other. They're different. And that's the most wonderful thing about the Bead Soup Blog Party. Now that I've seen what Nan made, I'm inspired to use filigree, and can't wait to make my first design.

—by Lori

Side Two

11 Cut five 2-in. (5cm) pieces of wire. On one piece, make a plain loop, connect it to the top textured ring on the top of the pendant. String a 10mm copper luster bead and make another plain loop. Make a chain of four linked 10mm copper luster bead units.

12 Make a plain loop at the end of a 2-in. wire and connect it to the last copper luster bead unit. String a 9x6mm blue Picasso Czech fire-polished rondelle. Make a plain loop above the bead.

13 Cut a 3-in. piece of wire. Make a plain loop, connecting it to the rondelle link. String a 12mm brass filigree bead cap, a 15mm handmade polymer clay bead, and a 12mm brass filigree bead cap. Make a plain loop.

14 Repeat Steps 8–10, but substitute the ring end of the toggle clasp.

Recipe
Earrings

1 On a beaded headpin, string a 6mm blue fire-polished round and a 7mm brass bead cap. Make a wrapped loop.

2 Cut a 2½-in. (6.4cm) piece of wire. Make a wrapped loop at one end, capturing the bead dangle you made in Step 1. String a 7mm brass bead cap, a 10mm blue Czech glass fire-polished round, and a 7mm brass bead cap. Make a wrapped loop to connect the dangle to the leverback earring wire.

3 Make a second earring.

Earrings

Ingredients
- **2** 10mm blue Czech fire-polished rounds
- **2** 6mm blue Czech fire-polished rounds
- **6** 7mm brass bead caps
- **2** 2-in. (5cm) brass headpins
- **5** in. (13cm) 22-gauge brass wire
- **2** brass lever back earring wires

Fine Dining

Ingredients
Bead Soup used from Barbara Lewis (Maryland)
32mm enameled wire ring focal, Barbara Lewis
2 20mm turquoise enameled beads, Barbara Lewis
4 14mm turquoise enameled beads, Barbara Lewis
2 12mm turquoise enameled beads, Barbara Lewis
32mm brass hook clasp, Cindy Wimmer

Bead Soup used from Cindy Wimmer's Pantry
6 15–30mm vintage earrings (dangles, posts, or clips)
16-in. strand (41cm) 7mm pale green and pale yellow
    mother-of-pearl rice beads
7 in. (18cm) brass oval rope chain, 10mm links
4 crimp beads
4 brass crimp covers
5 5mm oxidized brass jump rings
32 in. (81cm) 20-gauge oxidized brass wire
20 in. (51cm) beading wire

Utensils
-Roundnose pliers
-Chainnose pliers
-Flatnose pliers
-Crimping pliers
-Wire cutters
-Heavy-duty wire cutters
-Metal hole punch
-Metal file

This necklace is made with ingredients that epitomize fine dining. Vintage flowers, handmade enameled beads, and delicate mother-of-pearl beads make this necklace a taste treat. Don't have access to vintage flowers? Substitute your favorite gemstones or handmade beads. Who knows? Just as you might be pleasantly surprised when you try a new food, you might discover a new love for vintage shopping!

Recipe

1. Use heavy-duty wire cutters to cut posts or clips from the back of the vintage earrings. File the metal smooth. Use the hole punch to punch a hole about 3mm from the edge of each earring.

2. Cut a 7-in. (18cm) piece of chain. Open the center link and attach the enameled wire focal.

3. Use a 5mm jump ring to attach an earring three links from the pendant. Attach a total of three earrings on each side, three links apart.

4. Cut a 4-in. (10cm) piece of wire and make a plain loop on one end to create a eyepin. String an enameled bead and make the first half of a wrapped loop. Repeat for all of the 12mm and 14mm enameled beads. Attach a bead dangle evenly spaced between two earrings and complete the wraps. Repeat to attach all the dangles.

5. Cut a 4-in. piece of wire. Make a wrapped loop. String a 20mm enameled bead. Make the first half of a wrapped loop, connect to an end link of chain, and complete the wrap. Repeat on the other end of the chain.

6. Cut a 10-in. (25cm) piece of beading wire. String a crimp and the wrapped loop of a 20mm enameled bead. Go back through the crimp. Crimp the crimp bead and cover with a crimp cover. Repeat.

7. On one wire, string 7 in. (18cm) of light green mother-of-pearl rice beads. String a crimp and the clasp. Go back through the crimp. Crimp the crimp bead and cover with a crimp cover.

8. Repeat Step 7 with the light yellow mother-of-pearl rice beads, this time stringing 7¼ in. (18.4cm) of beads. The longer strand is the outside strand.

9. Hook the clasp into the wrapped loop of the 20mm enameled bead.

Roasted Eggplant with Chicken and Leeks Soup

By Jeannie Dukic (Minnesota)

Ingredients

Bead Soup used from Lori Anderson (Maryland)

35x35mm natural wood pendant
30x18mm antiqued copper butterfly pendant
8 16mm natural wood round beads
6 15mm green Czech glass flat square beads
10 10mm purple dyed Buri beads
8 8mm antiqued Thai-style copper beads
36 4mm corrugated antiqued copper rounds
22x22mm antiqued copper toggle clasp

Beads used from Jeannie Dukic's Pantry

2 copper crimp tubes
2 copper crimp covers
30 1¼-in. (3.2cm) antiqued copper headpins

20 in. (51cm) copper-colored beading wire
12 in. (30cm) 20-gauge antiqued copper wire

Utensils

- Roundnose pliers
- Flatnose pliers
- Crimping pliers
- Wire cutters
- Alligator clip

Not all jewelry has to be made with expensive components. This necklace is an example of how modest beads can create a beautiful piece with color, texture, and imagination. Subtle clusters of copper beads add a bit of excitement to the simple adornment of a wired butterfly on the wooden pendant. The added texture of the deep purple dyed Buri seeds are a beautiful blend with the smoothness of the natural wood and pale green Czech tablets. Bon appétit— on a budget!

Recipe

Make the Pendant

1 String the the butterfly on the 20-gauge copper wire, leaving a 1-in. (2.5cm) tail at the top. Center the butterfly on the wood pendant.

2 With the long end of the wire, wrap from the bottom to the top around the wood pendant, threading the wire through the copper butterfly with each pass.

3 When you're left with an inch or so of wire, bend the wire ends underneath existing wires at the back of wood pendant. With flatnose pliers, kink each wire in back of the wood pendant to tighten the wires and secure the butterfly pendant.

Make the Necklace

4 String a 4mm corrugated copper round onto a headpin and make a wrapped loop. Make 30 dangles.

5 Center the butterfly and wood pendant on the beading wire. Attach an alligator clip to one end of the beading wire.

6 On one end of the necklace, string: 8mm Thai-style copper bead, *wood bead, five 4mm dangles from Step 2. Repeat pattern two times from *. String: wood bead, 8mm copper bead, green bead, 8mm copper bead, green bead, 8mm copper bead, purple Buri bead, green bead. String: *purple Buri bead, 4mm corrugated copper bead. Repeat pattern two times from *. End with a purple Buri bead.

7 String a copper crimp tube and the small hole in the toggle clasp. Go back through the crimp tube and crimp. Cover the crimp tube with a copper crimp cover and trim the beading wire.

8 Remove the alligator clip. Repeat Steps 6 and 7 on the other end.

Tip Don't have copper crimp tubes? Use sterling silver and cover with copper crimp covers. No one will ever know!

Vintage Bean Soup

By Lori Anderson (Maryland)

Bead Soup used from Shannon LeVart (Missouri)
3 25mm 16-guage rings in violet patina, Shannon LeVart
4 16x9mm rondelles in dark purple patina, Shannon LeVart
4 14x5mm flower rondelles in violet patina, Shannon LeVart
2 15mm curved disks in pale blue patina, Shannon LeVart
2 15mm curved disks in lilac, Shannon LeVart
4 10mm salmon pink patina rounds, Shannon LeVart
4 8mm blue patina rounds, Shannon LeVart
26mm toggle in salmon pink patina, Shannon LeVart

Utensils
- *Roundnose pliers*
- *Chainnose pliers*
- *Flatnose pliers*
- *Wire cutters*

Beads used from Lori Anderson's Pantry
2 12mm mother-of-pearl large-hole buttons
12mm mother-of-pearl two-hole spangle button
16 12mm mother-of-pearl four-hole buttons
32 6mm dark pink glass flower petal beads
16 7mm 16-gauge sterling silver jump rings
5 4.5mm 16-gauge sterling silver jump rings (for pendant)
2 3mm 16-gauge sterling silver jump rings (for toggle)
2 2-in. (5cm) 22-gauge sterling silver headpins
20 in. (51cm) 20-gauge sterling silver wire

I remember shelling beans with my grandmother when I was little. I was particularly fascinated with the pink-and-white pods of runner beans fresh out of the garden—who knew beans could have such color and character? The quiet pleasure of sitting on her patio is a lovely memory. For this necklace, adding vintage mother-of-pearl buttons from my grandmother's stash to the muted patinated beads in the Bead Soup gives an unexpected visual appeal.

Recipe

Make the Pendant

1 Open a 4.5mm jump ring. String a 25mm violet ring, a 12mm large-hole button, and a 25mm violet ring. Close the jump ring.

2 On a 2-in. (5cm) headpin, string two 6mm petal beads. Make a wrapped loop, connecting it through the bottom large hole of the 12mm button.

3 Open two 4.5mm jump rings. String a jump ring through the previous 25mm violet ring, one hole in the two-hole spangle button, and through the remaining 25mm violet ring. Repeat with the second jump ring.

4 Open a 4.5mm jump ring and string through the violet 25mm ring and the top hole of a 12mm large-hole button. Close the jump ring. Make a dangle as in Step 2 and attach to this button.

5 Open a 4.5mm jump ring and string it through the jump ring attached in Step 4. Close the jump ring.

Make Bead Links

6 Cut four 2-in. pieces of wire. Make a wrapped-loop link with a petal bead, a 16x9mm dark purple rondelle, and a petal. Make a total of four links (A).

7 Cut a 3-in. (7.6cm) piece of wire. Make a wrapped-loop link with two 12mm four-hole buttons, a petal bead, a 15mm pale blue curved disk, a petal bead, and two 12mm four-hole buttons. Make two links with light blue curved disks (B) and two links with lilac curved disks (C).

Tip if your buttons have a pattern, string the buttons with the patterns facing outwards—not towards each other.

8 Cut four 2-in. pieces of wire. Make a wrapped-loop link with a petal bead, a 14x5mm violet flower rondelle, and a petal bead. Make a total of four links (D).

9 Cut four 2-in. pieces of wire. Make a wrapped-loop link with a 10mm salmon round. Make a total of four links (E).

10 Cut two 2-in. pieces of wire. Make a wrapped-loop link with a petal bead, an 8mm blue round, and a petal bead. Make a total of four links (F).

Assemble the Necklace

11 Open an 4.5mm jump ring and string an A, the top jump ring from the pendant, and another A. Close the jump ring.

12 Open 18 7mm jump rings.

13 Working on one side of the necklace, string a 7mm jump ring through the top wrapped loop of A and a wrapped loop of B. Close the jump ring. Continue connecting bead units together in the same manner, opening and closing the 7mm jump rings so one side of the necklace follows this pattern: A (from Step 1), B, D, E, A, C, F, D, E, and F.

14 Open a 3mm jump ring. String through the F unit and the bar of the toggle clasp. Close the jump ring.

15 Repeat Steps 13 and 14 for the other side of the necklace, substituting the toggle ring.

Earrings

Ingredients
2 15mm curved disks in tan patina, Shannon LeVart
2 10mm salmon pink patina rounds, Shannon LeVart
2 8mm blue patina rounds, Shannon LeVart
2 6mm dark pink glass flower petal bead
2 3-in. (7.6cm) 22-gauge sterling silver headpins
2 sterling silver earring wires

Recipe

1 On a 3-in. headpin, string a 10mm round, a petal bead, a tan curved disk, a petal, a 6mm round, and a petal bead. Make a wrapped loop.

2 Attach the earring wire.

3 Make a second earring.

CHAPTER FOUR
THE RANDOM PURCHASE METHOD

Time to go shopping!

This Bead Soup method is fun, but it requires you to force yourself away from your normal choices. If you're a pearl and crystal aficionado, try choosing ceramic or wood. If you only use sterling silver, choose copper or brass. Like new? Try vintage. Back away from the favorites, and search out new colors, styles, metals, and shapes.

Some examples:
❍ Before you go to your local bead store, decide you're going to buy something in a particular color—say, blue—and buy two strands of blue beads, then mix them up with beads you already own.

❍ Buy an outstanding toggle clasp and use it as a focal with something from your current bead stash.

❍ Trade favorite bead and component suppliers with a friend and discover new beads and findings.

The Silver Soup Spoon

By Lori Anderson (Maryland)

Ingredients

Bead Soup used from Cindy Wimmer (Virginia)

30mm Thai silver flower pendant
3 10mm Thai rectangle beads
2 10mm Thai rose charms
25mm Thai silver flower S-clasp

Beads used from Lori Anderson's Pantry

27x15mm pale green porcelain bird
22mm vintage diamond link
20mm large-hole purple ceramic disk bead
15mm coral flower
14mm faceted pale yellow polymer clay bead
10mm smooth amethyst rondelle
10mm sodalite barrel
4 10mm moonstone rondelles

3 7mm smooth turquoise rondelles
4 6mm smooth coral rondelles
3 6mm faceted amethyst rondelles
4 6mm purple Cebu Beauty shell beads
4 5mm faceted phrenite rondelles
5mm faceted garnet briolette
3mm sodalite round
2 3mm faceted amethyst rondelles

3 3mm smooth turquoise rondelles
3 8mm fancy daisy spacers
19 3mm daisy spacers
2 7mm 16-gauge sterling silver jump rings
2 4.5mm 16-gauge sterling silver jump rings
16 2.75mm 18-gauge sterling silver jump rings
5 2-in. (5cm) 22-gauge sterling silver headpins
5 in. (13cm) 5x4mm oval link chain
3 in. (7.6cm) 5x3mm patterned oval chain
1½ in. (3.8cm) fancy round link chain
36 in. (.9m) 22-gauge sterling silver wire, cut
 into 2-in. (5cm) pieces
6 in. (15cm) 22-gauge sterling silver wire, cut in half
2 in. (5cm) 24-gauge sterling silver wire

Utensils
- *Roundnose pliers*
- *Chainnose pliers*
- *Flatnose pliers*
- *Crimping pliers*
- *Wire cutters*

This all-metal soup features Thai silver. While flowers carry the theme in the soup cup, you can quickly see how versatile silver is. This monotone metal mix opens the door to all sorts of delicious concoctions. I created a necklace with a variety of colors and bead styles. Experiment with your own Bead Soup mix and favorite beads you've been hoarding for that special piece! A bracelet and a pair of earrings are perfect "side dishes" for your creative cooking with silver.

Recipe
Make the Pendant

1 Cut the chain: 1-in. (2.5cm) and ½-in. (1.3cm) pieces of fancy round link chain; 1½-in. (3.8cm) piece of patterned chain; 1½-in. piece of 5x4mm oval link chain.

2 Open two 7mm jump rings. On one jump ring, string an end link of all the chain pieces cut in Step 1. String the bail on the back of the rose pendant. Close the jump ring. String the other jump ring through the bail opening and close the jump ring. This ring will be the foundation for the rest of the necklace.

3 Make four dangles:
On a 2-in. (5cm) headpin, string:
   a. a 3mm sodalite round and a 3mm spacer
   b. a 6mm amethyst rondelle and a 5mm phrenite rondelle
   c. a 3mm turquoise rondelle and a 3mm spacer

On a 2-in. piece of 24-gauge sterling silver wire:
   d. make a briolette wrap above the 5mm faceted garnet briolette

4 Make a wrapped loop above the beads and connect each dangle to the bottom link of a chain dangling from the rose pendant.

BACK OF PENDANT

Necklace Side One

5 Use 2-in. pieces of wire to make wrapped-loop links:
   a. String a 6mm faceted amethyst rondelle, a 3mm spacer, and 3mm turquoise rondelle. Connect one end of the link to the rose pendant before completing the wraps.
   b. String a 3mm spacer, three moonstone rondelles, and a 3mm spacer. Use a 2.75mm jump ring to connect this link to the link made in "a."
   c. String the coral rose. Use a 2.75mm jump ring to connect this link to the link made in "b." Use a 2.75mm jump ring to connect the rose link to the end link of a 1-in. piece of 5x4mm oval link chain.

6 String a phrenite rondelle on a headpin and make the first half of a wrapped loop. Connect the end link of the chain piece and complete the wrapped loop. Attach a Thai silver rose charm to the end chain link with a jump ring. With a 2-in. piece of wire, make a wrapped loop, stringing it through the jump ring before completing the wrap. String a 3mm spacer, a 6mm amethyst rondelle, and a 3mm spacer. Make a wrapped loop. Connect a 2.75mm jump ring through the loop.

7 On a headpin, string a 3mm amethyst rondelle, string it through the bottom loop of the amethyst bead link from Step 6, and complete the wrap.

8 With a 2-in. piece of wire, make a wrapped-loop link with a 3mm spacer, the porcelain bird, and a 3mm spacer. Connect the bird link to the amethyst link made in Step 6 with a jump ring.

9 With a 2-in. piece of wire, make a wrapped-loop link with a Cebu Beauty shell, an 8mm spacer, and a shell. Connect the shell link to the bird link with a jump ring.

10 With a 2-in. piece of wire, make a wrapped-loop link with a 3mm spacer, a sodalite barrel, and a 3mm spacer. Connect the sodalite link to the shell link with a jump ring.

11 Connect a hole in the 22mm diamond link with the sodalite link using a 4.5mm jump ring.

12 With a 2-in. piece of wire, make a wrapped-loop link with a coral rondelle, a 3mm spacer, two coral rondelles, a moonstone rondelle, and a coral rondelle. Use a 2.75mm jump ring to connect this link to the remaining hole in the 22mm vintage diamond link.

13 With a 2-in. piece of wire, make a wrapped-loop link with a 3mm spacer, a 10mm amethyst rondelle and a phrenite rondelle. Use a 2.75mm jump ring to connect this link to the coral link.

14 With a 2-in. piece of wire make a wrapped-loop link with a 3mm spacer, a 10mm Thai silver rectangle, and a 3mm spacer. Use a 2.75mm jump ring to connect this link to the amethyst link, and another jump ring to connect it to the ring half of the S-clasp.

Necklace Side Two

15 With a 2-in. piece of wire, make the first half of a wrapped loop, connect it to the 7mm jump ring of the rose pendant, and complete the wraps. String two purple Cebu Beauty shells. Make a wrapped loop.

16 With a 2-in. piece of wire, make a wrapped-loop link with a 3mm spacer, a sodalite barrel, and a 3mm spacer. Use a 2.75mm jump ring to connect the sodalite link and the shell link.

17 With a 2-in. piece of wire, make a wrapped-loop link with a 3mm turquoise rondelle, a 10mm Thai silver rectangle bead, and a 3mm spacer. Use a 2.75mm jump ring to connect the link to the sodalite link.

18 Cut a 3-in. piece of 22-gauge wire. String it through an 8mm spacer, the large hole in the purple ceramic disk, and through another 8mm spacer. Bend the wire in a U-shape with equal ends. Make a briolette wrap and a wrapped loop. Use a 2.75mm jump ring to connect the loop with the silver rectangle link.

19 Repeat Step 4 on the other half of the bead and connect to an end link of the 1½ in. patterned chain.

20 Open a 2.75mm jump ring and pick up a Thai silver rose charm and the end link of the patterned chain. Close the jump ring.

21 With a 2-in. piece of wire, make a wrapped-loop link with yellow polymer clay bead. Open a 2.75mm jump ring, string the rose charm from Step 6, the end link of chain from Step 5, and the end loop of the yellow bead link. Close the jump ring.

22 With a 2-in. piece of wire, make a wrapped loop. String a 3mm amethyst rondelle, a Thai silver barrel, and a phrenite rondelle. Make the first half of a wrapped loop. Use a 2.75mm jump ring to connect the completed loop and the yellow bead link. On the unfinished wrap, string the end link of the 2.5mm 5x4mm oval link chain. Complete the wraps.

23 With a 2-in. piece of wire, make a wrapped loop, first stringing it through the end link of the previous chain. String a 3mm spacer, three 7mm turquoise rondelles, and a 3mm spacer. Make a wrapped loop. Use a 2.75mm jump ring to connect the link to the rose half of the S-clasp.

Mixed Metal Bracelet & Earrings

Sometimes I run out of silver and have to resort to other things. This bracelet mixes Thai silver with antiqued brass. Mixing metals is a creative way to give a design extra distinction. Use 5x3mm oval link sterling silver chain and wire wrap charms on antiqued brass headpins. Use the Thai rectangles from the Bead Soup with Purple Velvet and Fuchsia Swarovski crystals and a piece of vintage chain with opalescent sea-green beads. A simple sterling silver toggle keeps the focus on the unique quality of the bracelet.

The mixed-metal earrings match the bracelet and are a fun combination of beads and vintage chain. Cap the silver hour-glass beads with 3mm Purple Velvet and Fuchsia Swarovski crystal beads. A four-bead length of beaded chain loops onto sterling silver jump rings, and the 8mm purple velvet Swarovski crystals capture both links in the bottom of the chain.

The Golden Consommé of Aquitaine

By Cindy Wimmer (Virginia)

Ingredients
Bead Soup used from Lori Anderson (Maryland)

89mm vermeil tassel
25mm vermeil hook clasp
2 12x6mm vermeil marquis-shaped beads
2 11mm vermeil hexagon beads
16 4mm tourmaline beads
4 ft. (1.2m) of 26-gauge gold-filled wire
16 in. (41cm) 2.3mm gold-filled long-and-short link chain
16 in. (41cm) 2.7mm gold-filled flat textured oval chain
12 in. (30cm) 22-gauge gold-filled wire
10½ in. (25cm) vermeil round link chain

Beads used from Cindy Wimmer's Pantry

24 4mm faceted peridot rondelles
24 3.5mm faceted apatite rondelles
1½ in. (3.8cm) 5mm gold-filled textured cable chain

This elegant, regal necklace is fit for dining in the finest Parisian restaurants. The soup begins with a mix of vermeil beads and chain. The challenge with an all-metal soup mix is to give it a distinctive flavor and taste all its own. For this necklace, Cindy chose to create a queenly palette of fine gemstones mixed with delicate chain. What would you do with a handful of golden beads?

Utensils
- *Roundnose pliers*
- *Chainnose pliers*
- *Flatnose pliers*
- *Crimping pliers*
- *Wire cutters*

Recipe

1 Create seven jump rings from the 5mm textured chain by opening each link. Set aside.

2 Cut eight 2-in. (5cm) pieces of the long-and-short chain and of flat oval chain.

3 Create chains of two-rondelle units: Cut a 3-in. (7.6cm) piece of 26-gauge wire. Make a wrapped loop. String two peridot rondelles. Make a wrapped loop above the beads. Make a second unit with two tourmaline beads, attaching one wrapped loop through peridot link and competing both sets of wraps. Continue in this manner to link an apatite unit and another peridot unit. Complete the last set of wraps. Make four identical strands.

4 Repeat Step 3, but connect links in this order: apatite, peridot, tourmaline, and apatite. Make four identical strands.

5 Using a jump ring from Step 1, connect one piece of each chain style from Step 2 and one strand from Step 3 to the loop of the tassel.

6 Cut a 3-in. piece of 22-gauge wire. Make the first half of a wrapped loop, connect it to each piece of chain and the gemstone strand, and complete the wraps. String a vermeil hexagon bead. Make the first half of a wrapped loop above the bead, connect two chain pieces and a gemstone strand, and complete the wraps.

7 Cut a nine-link piece of round link chain. Loosely twist the three strands, and with a jump ring, attach them to the round link chain.

8 Open a jump ring and attach to the end link of the round link chain. Attach a long-and-short piece of chain, a flat oval piece of chain, and a gemstone strand from Step 4. Close the jump ring. Repeat Step 6, attaching a vermeil marquis bead to the piece of chain.

9 Twist the long-and-short chain, flat oval chain, and gemstone strand loosely. Open a jump ring and attach the chains and the hook clasp. Close the jump ring.

10 Repeat Steps 5–9 to create the other half of the necklace.

Savory Tomato Soup

By Kerry Bogert (New York)

Ingredients

Bead Soup used from Lori Anderson (Maryland)
Sterling silver three-circle pendant (rings measure 42mm, 27mm, 23mm)
4 12mm sterling silver coin-shaped beads
20 6mm red faceted Czech glass rondelles
20mm sterling silver toggle

Beads used from Kerry Bogert's Pantry
4 21mm lampworked glass lentil beads, Kerry Bogert
10 8mm lampworked glass headpins, Kerry Bogert
20 2-in. (5cm) sterling silver headpins
4 3mm jump rings (optional)
18 in. (45cm) 2.7mm gunmetal rolo chain
60 in. (1.5m) 20-gauge sterling silver wire
72 in. (1.8m) 22-gauge red-colored copper wire

Utensils
- Roundnose pliers
- Chainnose pliers
- Wire cutters

Peppered with red and black, this sterling silver and glass design has over-the-top drama and appeal that makes it an extra-savory dish. This is an excellent example of using a pendant creatively. By deconstructing the connected pendant into three component parts, the necklace enjoys a completely new look.

Recipe

1 Using chainnose pliers, open the jump rings connecting the three circles of the pendant. Separate the pendant into three pieces. Set the jump rings aside for later.

2 Leaving a 3-in. tail, wrap a 12-in. (30cm) piece of red wire around the edge of the 42mm silver pendant circle three times on one side of the hole, creating two wire tails. Twist the two tails together tightly against the wrapped edge and make a wrapped loop.

3 Repeat Step 2 on the other side of the pendant's hole.

4 Repeat Steps 2 and 3 with the remaining two silver pendant circles.

5 Cut four 3-in. pieces of sterling silver wire. Make a lampworked bead wrapped-loop link connecting the large pendant circle with one of the smaller circles. Repeat on the other end. Connect another lampworked bead wrapped-loop link on each end.

6 Cut four 3-in. pieces of sterling silver wire. Make a wrapped-loop link with a silver disk bead and connect it to an end lampworked bead link from Step 5. Repeat on the other end and once more on each end.

7 String a red Czech glass bead onto a headpin. Make a plain loop above the bead. Make a total of 20 dangles.

8 Using one of the jump rings saved in Step 1, string five dangles onto the jump ring and connect the jump ring to the bottom hole of the largest silver ring. String five dangles on another jump ring and connect it to the top hole in the largest silver ring.

9 Repeat Step 8 for the smaller silver rings, this time only adding one set of five dangles to the outer holes in the rings.

10 Cut the chain into two 9-in. (23cm) pieces. Open an end link on one chain piece and attach it to the end wrapped loop on one end of the necklace. Close the link. Repeat on the other end.

Tip If your chain's links are soldered, use a small jump ring to connect the chain to the wrapped loop.

11 Make a plain loop on each lampworked headpin. Attach five headpin dangles to one side of the chain, about six links apart from each other. Repeat on the other side.

12 Connect the clasp components to each end of the chain by opening and closing the last link of the chain or using jump rings.

Soup at the Bistro

By Lori Anderson (Maryland)

Ingredients
64mm Thai silver tube bead with seven loops
15mm Bali silver charm
2 10mm white cultured pearls
6 10mm assorted Bali silver beads
14 8mm faceted onyx beads
9 8mm round Swarovski crystal rounds, Crystal Silver Shade
2 4.25mm 16-gauge sterling silver jump rings
6 2½-in. (6.4cm) 22-gauge sterling silver headpins
4 4mm sterling silver crimp tube ends with top loops
88 in. (2.2m) 22-gauge sterling silver wire
32 in. (81cm) black Greek leather
25mm marcasite toggle

Utensils
- *Roundnose pliers*
- *Chainnose pliers*
- *Wire cutters*

This necklace is truly a piece that can be worn anywhere—your favorite local bistro over a t-shirt and jeans or an elegant soiree uptown at a posh restaurant. The unexpected neckline of black leather helps make this pearl, crystal, and silver necklace less stringent and straight-laced. The black onyx mixes well with the leather, but you could just as easily substitute any color you like! This is an example of what to do when you buy a component (in my instance, a looped bead tube) and then wonder why you bought it and what in the world to do with it. Search through your bead stash and find a piece that's been sitting in a corner languishing, and get cooking!

Recipe

1 Cut 36 2½-in. (6.4cm) pieces of 22-gauge wire.

2 Using beaded wrapped-loop links, connect the following to the tube bead, from right to left:

   a. pearl, Bali bead, pearl, onyx, pearl, crystal (on a 22-gauge headpin).
   b. onyx, crystal, onyx, crystal, Bali bead, onyx (on a 22-gauge headpin).
   c. crystal, pearl, Bali bead, onyx, crystal, pearl (on a 22-gauge headpin).
   d. pearl, onyx, onyx, crystal, pearl, onyx, Bali charm.
   e. onyx, Bali bead, pearl, Bali bead, onyx, crystal (on a 22-gauge headpin).
   f. crystal, pearl, onyx, crystal, onyx, pearl (on a 22-gauge headpin).
   g. pearl, onyx, crystal, Bali bead, pearl, onyx (on a 22-gauge headpin).

3 Cut two 16-in. (41cm) pieces of leather. On each end, use chainnose pliers to crimp a crimp end (this style of crimp is flat-crimped in the center). String the leather strands through the silver tube bead.

4 Use a 4.25mm jump ring to connect two crimp-end loops to the loop of the toggle ring. Close the ring. Repeat on the other end, substituting the toggle bar.

Earrings

String a 10mm white pearl on a headpin. Make a wrapped loop. Make a wrapped-loop link with an onx bead, connecting it to the white pearl section. Make a wrapped-loop link with a crystal, connecting it to the onyx bead section. Connect the dangle to the earring wire. Make a second earring.

Substitute

Want to add some glitz to your wardrobe? Use the same style tube bead and string a cornucopia of 4mm Swarovski crystal bicones, connecting them at random loops on the tube and using chain instead of leather. Affordable bling!

Fruit Compote

By Stefanie Teufel (Germany)

Ingredients
Bead Soup used from Lori Anderson (Maryland)
(Note: The fruit beads are all between 10–15mm)

10 apple beads
7 banana beads
6 yellow lemon beads
5 pear beads
4 nut beads
4 dark blue grape beads
4 green grape beads
3 strawberry beads
3 red grape beads
3 purple grape beads

orange grape bead
green lime bead
blue grape bead
45mm sterling silver curved bead
2 30mm sterling silver curved bead
2 25mm sterling silver curved beads
2 20mm sterling silver curved beads
22mm sterling silver grape clasp (ring portion only)

Beads from Stefanie Teufel's Pantry
15mm round metal ring
15mm square metal ring
2 sterling silver crimp tubes
2 sterling silver crimp covers
20 in. (51cm) green sari silk ribbon
20 in. (51cm) flexible beading wire

Utensils
- Chainnose pliers
- Crimping pliers
- Wire cutters
- Fray Check (optional)

A fruit compote is a bit like a stew but oh-so-much-better than vegetable stew in my opinion! The fun glass fruit beads are delightful and charming, and the sterling silver beads remind me of serving bowls.

Tip Sometimes a toggle bar is too short to keep the clasp closed, but don't despair—use the toggle ring as a charm holder.

Recipe

1 Cut 24 in. (61cm) of beading wire. String a crimp bead and the silver square. Go back through the crimp bead and crimp. Cover with a crimp cover.

2 String a banana and a 20mm curved bead.

3 String: apple, nut, lemon, banana, pear, dark blue grape, pear, and red grape. String a 25mm curved bead.

4 String: dark blue grape, apple, green grape, pear, banana, apple, lemon, and red grape. String a 30mm curved bead.

5 String: purple grape, strawberry, apple, lime, green grape, lemon, apple, and orange grape. String a 45mm curved bead.

6 String: strawberry, purple grape, nut, banana, green grape, lemon, nut, and apple. String a 30mm curved bead.

7 String: green grape, apple, pear, dark blue grape, pear, apple, banana, and lemon. String a 25mm curved bead.

8 String: apple, nut, dark blue grape, purple grape, lemon, apple, strawberry, and banana. String a 20mm curved bead.

9 String a banana. String a crimp bead and the round ring. Go back through the crimp bead and crimp. Cover with a crimp cover.

10 Knot a sari silk ribbon to each end.

11 At one end of the sari silk, knot through the larger ring of the clasp.

12 Attach an 8mm jump ring to the larger hole of the clasp and string a blue grape bead and a red grape bead.

13 Close the necklace with a bow.

Blue Onion Soup

By Libby Leuchtman (Missouri)

Ingredients

Bead Soup used from Lori Anderson (Maryland)

21mm blue and cream ceramic Kazuri bead

17 8mm blue Czech glass faceted rondelles

1¼-in. (3.2cm) Thai silver toggle clasp

Beads used from Libby Leuchtman's Pantry

30mm handmade lampworked cylinder bead, Libby Leuchtman

18x9mm handmade lampworked bead, Libby Leuchtman

12x9mm handmade lampworked bead, Libby Leuchtman

3 16-in. (41cm) strands of seed beads in various sizes, 6º–10º (round and triangular), in olive, dark blue, and cream

12 17mm aqua Czech glass ovals

2 11mm Bali sterling silver beads

12 8mm flat sterling silver beads

34 4mm olive green faceted Czech glass rondelles

4 10mm sterling silver daisy spacers

48 5mm cream glass spacers

10mm flat sterling silver ring

20mm fringed leaf chain

3 30-in. (76cm) pieces of flexible beading wire

2 3x3mm sterling silver crimp beads

3 in. 20-gauge sterling silver wire

Utensils

- Roundnose pliers
- Chainnose pliers
- Flatnose pliers
- Metal punch
- Crimping pliers
- Wire cutters
- File
- Heavy-duty cutters

Blue onion soup is an unusual soup made with bleu cheese. This is a good name for this soup mix (color aside!) because it's made with unusual beads. Kazuri beads are Kenyan free-trade ceramic beads that have a lovely history and beautiful patterns. They are available in many different colors and designs. Note the creative use of the toggle clasp—the bar turns into earrings, and the toggle ring becomes a lariat ring! It just goes to show you that findings can always be looked at in a fresh way.

Tip Thai silver is softer than sterling silver and works better for this project.

Recipe
Construct the Lariat Ring

1 Trim the small loop from the back of the toggle ring with the heavy-duty wire cutters, nipping as close to the ring as possible. File until the ends are smooth.

2 Using a metal punch, punch a hole about 2–3mm from the outer edge of the toggle ring. File away any burs.

String the Necklace

3 Onto all three strands of beading wire, string a crimp bead, 10 8º seed beads, and the toggle ring. Go back through the crimp bead, and crimp.

4 String an 11mm Bali silver bead, the 18x9mm lampworked bead, a 10mm spacer, a 21mm blue and cream ceramic Kazuri bead, and a 10mm spacer.

5 Separate the beading wire strands and work on each separately:

First strand: String five 6º cube beads, an 8mm Czech bead, a 10mm Czech bead, an 8mm Czech bead. Repeat to end.

Second strand: String seven 6º seed beads, a 6mm Czech rondelle, a 15mm Czech glass bead, a 6mm Czech rondelle. Repeat to end.

Third strand: String 15 8º seed beads, a 6mm rondelle bead, a 8mm Bali bead, and a 6mm rondelle bead. Repeat to the end.

When you have finished all three strands, you might have to add or subtract beads to make them even.

6 Over all three strands, string a Bali bead, a handmade lampworked glass bead, a Bali silver spacer, a crimp bead, and a 10mm silver ring. Go back through the crimp with all three strands and crimp. Cover with a crimp cover if desired.

7 Connect a 3-in. (7.6cm) piece of sterling silver wire to the 10mm silver ring with a wrapped loop. String a silver spacer, the 30mm handmade lampworked cylinder bead, and a spacer on the wire. Make the first half of a wrapped loop, connect the 20mm fringed leaf chain, and complete the wrapped loop.

Earrings

Using heavy-duty wire cutters, snip the toggle bar in half. Punch a small hole in one bar. File any rough edges or burs. Make a wrapped loop through the hole. String a spacer, a blue seed bead, a Kazuri bead, and a spacer. Make another wrapped loop. Attach an earring wire. Make a second earring.

Tip Always file in one direction.

Autumn Harvest Soup

By Barbara Lewis (Florida)

Ingredients

Bead Soup from Lori Anderson (Maryland)
32x32mm fossilized copper-dipped leaf
2 10mm faceted blue AB Czech glass beads
Copper toggle

Beads from Barbara Lewis' Bead Stash
(all enamel components by Barbara Lewis)
70mm vintage copper flower
35mm yellow enamel filigree flower
16mm etched copper disk bead
6mm rhinestone rondelle
6mm antiqued bronze bead
3mm brass heishi bead

3mm antiqued bronze bead
10mm antiqued bronze flat scalloped bead cap
8mm enameled bead cap, red and orchid
3 6mm 20-gauge copper jump rings
2 4mm copper heishi beads
8° glass seed bead
2 twisty tendrils 5-in. (13cm) double-dipped headpins
3 2½-in. (64 mm) white enamel headpins
3 9mm copper 20-gauge jump rings
26 in. (66cm) brass 3mm link chain, dark red
10 in. (25 mm) brass 3mm link chain, dark blue
13 in. bronze chain
5 in. (13cm) royal blue sari ribbon

Utensils

- Roundnose pliers
- Chainnose pliers
- Wire cutters
- Needle file
- Metal shears or disk cutter
- Ball peen hammer
- Two-hole metal punch
- File
- Scissors

Autumn. My favorite time of year. The crispness in the air, the proximity to the holidays, and the guarantee of a pot of soup simmering in the kitchen for dinner. For me, the first herald of autumn is the falling of the leaves. This copper-dipped leaf reminds me of days of endless raking, poking through the gardens for those last flowers of the season, and bright blue skies.

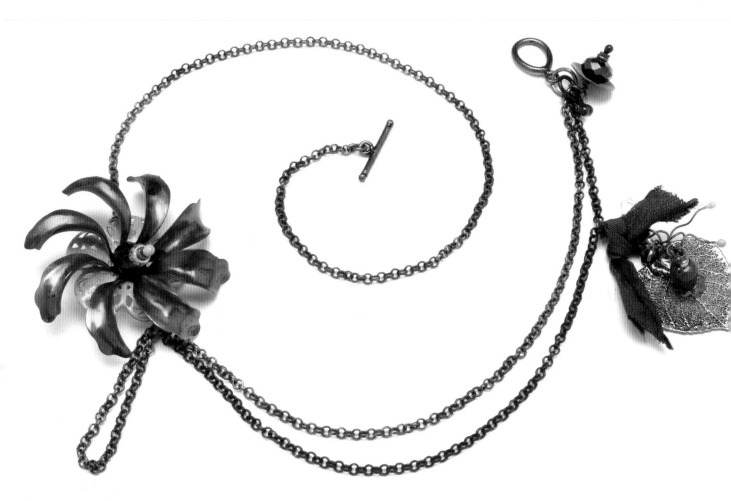

Recipe
Leaf Component

1. String a 10mm flat bead cap, a 6mm antique bronze bead, an 8mm enameled bead cap, and an 8º seed bead on a white enamel headpin. Make a wrapped loop above the beads.

2. Spiral the double-dipped headpins around roundnose pliers to create grapevine-like tendrils.

3. Cut a 2-in. (5cm) piece of dark blue chain. Open a jump ring, and connect the leaf, the dangle, and the tendrils to the chain. Close the jump ring. Wrap sari ribbon around the chain at the top of the copper leaf to conceal connections.

Flower Component

4. On an enamel headpin, string a copper heishi, rondelle, abacus bead, copper flower, and yellow enamel filigree flower. String a rondelle and a 3mm metal bead onto the headpin, and flatten the bead with chainnose pliers to crimp. Trim any excess headpin wire and file smooth.

Bead Dangle

5. With metal shears or a disk cutter, cut a 16mm disk from the etched copper. Punch a hole in the center of the disk with the silver-handled end of a two-hole metal punch. Gently cup the disk by hammering the back of the metal with a ball peen hammer. On an enamel headpin, string a 3mm heishi, a 4mm heishi, an abacus bead, and the copper disk. Make a wrapped loop above the beads. Bend a double-dipped headpin into a U-shape and string it through the loop. Cross the ends and pinch tight.

Assemble the Necklace

6 Connect an end-link of chain on the leaf component to the remaining 8-in. (20cm) section of dark blue chain with a jump ring 1 in. (2.5cm) from the end.

7 Cut a 9-in. (23cm) and a 4-in. (10cm) piece of dark red chain. Open a jump ring and connect the 9-in. red chain and the end of the blue chain to an opening in the bottom edge of the flower. Fold the 4-in. red chain in half, and connect at the two end links. Close the jump ring.

8 With a jump ring, connect the loop of the toggle clasp, the bead dangle, and the remaining ends of red and blue chains.

9 With a jump ring, connect the bronze chain to the top of the flower. Attach the toggle bar to the other end with a jump ring.

Enchanted Autumn Bracelet

Ingredients
3 10mm faceted abacus beads with aurora borealis finish
6 3mm heishi beads
3 2½-in. (6.4cm) enamel headpins
Assorted enamel bead caps (Barbara Lewis)
Metal adjustable bracelet
10mm jump ring
20 in. (51cm) sari ribbon
20 in. yarn

Utensils
- Roundnose pliers
- Chainnose pliers
- Wire cutters
- Scissors

Bracelet

1 Cut a 10-in. (25cm) piece of sari ribbon and wrap it around the center of the bracelet. Tie.

2 With assorted beads and bead caps, create three bead dangles on enamel headpins. Finish wire with a loop.

3 String all three dangles onto the jump ring. Close the jump ring over the center of the bracelet.

4 Wrap the bracelet with sari ribbon and yarn. The fiber wrappings control the bead placement, so you may need to experiment a bit to get things exactly the way you want them.

By Diane Cook (Texas)

Old-Fashioned Oyster Stew

Ingredients
Bead Soup used by Lori Anderson (Maryland)
40x30mm vintage cameo with brass setting
16 10mm white freshwater pearls
18 4mm green freshwater pearls
Oxidized bronze clasp

Beads used from Diane Cook's Pantry
10mm faceted crystal round, Topaz AB
3 10mm oxidized brass puffy heart charms
6mm oxidized brass daisy bead cap
2-in. (5cm) 22-gauge oxidized brass eye pin
18 26-gauge oxidized brass headpins (to fit pearls)
20 4mm 22-gauge oxidized brass jump rings
32 6.5mm 22-gauge oxidized brass jump rings
15 in. (38cm) 4x3mm oxidized brass small cable chain (optional)
8 ft. (24cm) 22-gauge bronze wire

Utensils
- *Roundnose pliers*
- *Flatnose pliers*
- *Chainnose pliers*
- *Flush Cutters*
- *Steel wool or 320 grit sanding pad (optional)*

For many, holidays aren't the same without traditional oyster stew. Everyone dresses up for dinner, relatives come from afar, and a lovely time is had by all. This necklace is made with a vintage cameo pin, freshwater pearls, and brass hearts. Its grace and beauty are the perfect accompaniment to a sumptuous special-occasion dinner.

Recipe

1 Cut 16 6-in. (15cm) pieces of bronze wire.

2 Make a wrapped-loop link with a white pearl and a piece of wire. Repeat to make 16 pearl links. If desired, use a sanding pad or steel wool to remove a bit of the patina from each of the wrapped loops.

3 Use two 6.25mm jump rings to connect two pearl links. Repeat to make two 8-link strands.

4 Connect one eight-pearl strand to one side of the cameo with two 6.25mm jump rings. Repeat with the other strand.

5 Connect the end of an eight-pearl strand to one half of the clasp with a 4mm jump ring. Repeat with the other strand.

6 String a 4mm green pearl onto a headpin and make a wrapped loop above the bead. Make 13 dangles.

7 Use a 4mm jump ring to attach a pearl dangle between the second and third white pearl links. Repeat to attach a total of three dangles. Repeat on the other strand in the same location.

8 Use a 4mm jump ring to attach a pearl dangle between the first and second white pearl links. Repeat to attach two dangles. Repeat on the other strand in the same location.

9 Use a 4mm jump ring to attach a heart between the two pearl dangles attached in Step 8. Repeat on the other strand in the same location.

Make the Cameo Dangle

10 String a 10mm crystal and the beadcap onto an eyepin. Make a wrapped loop to connect the dangle to the cameo.

11 Use a 4mm jump ring to attach a pearl dangle to the top loop between the crystal and the cameo. Repeat to add three dangles.

12 Connect a heart to the eye below the crystal with a 4mm jump ring.

Optional Toggle Adornment

13 Connect the 15-in. (38cm) piece of cable chain to the inside of the clasp using the 4mm jump rings attached in Step 5 (one on each side). This will make an accent strand or it becomes a way to lengthen the necklace.

14 String a 4mm green pearl onto a headpin and make the first half of a wrapped loop. Make five. Connect each dangle to a link of the middle section of the cable chain and complete the wraps. Space each dangle about three links apart on the chain, starting in the center and working towards the ends.

Tip Use Novacan Black or Liver of Sulfer according to the manufacturer's instructions to oxidize the wire before beginning the project. Some oxidizers can damage pearls.

Earrings

String a 10mm crystal and a 6mm bead cap onto an eyepin. Make a wrapped loop above the beads. String a pearl onto a headpin. Make a wrapped loop, attaching it to the eye of the eye pin. Connect a 10mm heart to the bottom of the dangle with a 4mm jump ring. Attach the earring wire. Make a second earring.

GALLERY

Ceclia Cormer
thebeadingyogini.com
The Turquoise Trail
Beads from Carol Bradley

Jess Italia Lincoln
vintaj.com
Breaking Waves
Beads from Lori Greenberg

Claire Maunsell
stillpointworks.blogspot.com
Enclosed
Beads from Cherrie Fick

Christine Damm
storiestheytell.blogspot.com
Silk Road
Beads from Shannon LeVarte

Ceclia Cormer
thebeadingyogini.com
The Dirty Martini
Beads from Carol Bradley

Heather Pyle
aquariart-chocoholic.blogspot.com
Spring's Promise, New Life
Beads from Angela Rae

Jennifer Heynen
jenniferjangles.com
Spiked Soup
Beads from Jenni Connolly

Joanna Matuszczyk
filcowe.blogspot.com
Cupidos
Beads from Courtney Breul

Regina Sannterre
reginaswritings.blogspot.com
Bayou Blue
Beads from Rose Binoya

Mary Ellen Parker
beetreebyme.etsy.com
Autumn Garden
Beads from Melissa Meman

Laura Zeiner
sticklizarddesigns.etsy.com
A Day at the Beach
Beads from Marcy Lamberson

Valorie Norton
hot-fused-glass.com
Bohemian Beaky Bird
Beads from Stephanie Haussler

Raida Disbrow
havanabeads.blogspot.com
Wondrous
Beads from Rebecca Watkins

Kathleen Robinson-Young
uglyducklingbeads.etsy.com
Soups On!
Beads from Cristi Clothier

ABOUT THE AUTHOR

Lori Anderson has led a wildly diverse life that had nothing to do with creativity until she was introduced to beads in 2002. She was a Korean linguist for the U.S. Air Force, a pre-med biology graduate of the University of Virginia, a sales and marketing professional for the high-tech industry during the dot.com boom, and now, a wife, mother, and full-time jewelry artist. Her style is as varied and eclectic as the life she's led. You can find her work at LoriAnderson.net and visit her blog and join her Bead Soup Blog Parties at PrettyThingsBlog.com. She currently resides on the eastern shore of Maryland.

Designers and Handmade Bead Contributors

Rebecca Anderson

Rebecca is a jewelry designer from the U.K. She's been making jewelry since she was a little girl and able to thread beads. She added bead weaving as a teenager and later expanded her repertoire to include wirework, bead embroidery, and metal work. She is a three time-finalist and two-time winner in the British Bead Awards and was voted Beads and Beyond Readers' Designer of the Year in 2011. See her work at *SongBead.etsy.com*.

Zachary Anderson

Zachary, Lori Anderson's nine-year old son, has been fascinated with color since he was a baby and his mom took him to yarn stores and art museums. An artist in his own right, his artwork has been exhibited at the Art Academy in Easton, Md. He would love to go to art school, but only if his mom goes too.

Barbara Bechtel

Barbara's art encompasses several different media, including jewelry and bead design, mixed media painting, bookmaking, and assemblage. Inspired by old things, history, and nature, her work tells a story. Barbara holds a bachelor of fine arts degree in painting from the Savannah College of Art and Design. She lives and works full time from her home studio in Merritt Island, Fla. For more, visit *secondsurf.com*.

Kerry Bogert

Kerry Bogert is a mom, author, artist, and designer living in western New York state with her husband and three children. When she isn't making lampworked glass beads, she's coming up with new ways to show off her beads in colorful, creative jewelry. She is the author of *Totally Twisted* and *Rustic Wrappings*. See more of her work at *KabsConcepts.com*.

Melanie Brooks

Melanie began Earthenwood Studio when she decided to combine her love of ceramics and jewelry making and become a porcelain bead maker. Over the years, she has sold her handcrafted ceramic jewelry, beading components, and ceramic gift tiles at galleries, bead stores, and trade shows all over the country. View Melanie's work at *EarthenwoodStudio.com, Earthenwood.etsy.com*, and *EarthenwoodCeramics.etsy.com*.

Jennifer Cameron

Creating with fire since 2005, Jennifer discovered jewelry making after realizing a small child could easily disappear in the growing collection of beads sitting around her house. She is the adoring mother of two, jackpot winner in the husband category, and the zookeeper of several pets. You can find her work at *GlassAddictions.com*.

Diane Cook

Diane Cook, mixed-media artist, teaches internationally at popular art retreats. Her artistic journey, started as a whim more than seven years ago, has developed into a full-time passion. Her love for using vintage jewelry has become an ever-constant source of inspiration. Additional loves include photography and mixed-media art. Diane has been published in many magazines and was a guest curator for *Crescendoh.com*, sharing her story for *Art Saves* in May, 2010.

Christine Damm

Christine Damm can't remember a time in her life when she was not drawing or sewing or doing something with her hands. She has been a potter, a dressmaker, a textile designer, and a graphic artist. Christine is also a storyteller and believes as our lives tell a story, so does our art. Christine studied art at New York University and The School for American Craftsmen at the Rochester Institute of Technology.

Malin de Koning

Malin de Koning is a former graphic/industrial/web designer and artist who turned to jewelry making in 2008. She loves exploring and learning new things and finding exciting, appetizing combinations of materials and colors. Malin lives with her English husband, their two children, and two ginger cats in a small house in the countryside just outside Stockholm, Sweden. View more of Malin's work at *MalindeKoning.etsy.com*.

Cassie Donlen

Cassie has been a lampwork artist and jewelry designer since 2001. She lives in St. Louis, Mo., with her fab husband and three rockin' sons. Needless to say, she never has a dull moment. She is the author and creator of *Lampworking with Cassie Donlen*, a lampworking how-to DVD. You can buy her beads and jewelry at *GlassBeadle.com*.

Jeannie Dukic
Jeannie lives in Minnesota with her husband, daughter and lots of animals. She's a self-taught jewelry designer, polymer clay and mixed media artist, and instructor. Her artwork has been displayed in many juried art fairs. She is a graduate of St. Paul Collage of Visual Arts. Find her at *JKDJewelry.com* or *site.jkdjewelry.com/blog*.

Nan Emmett
Nan Emmett is a full time ceramic artist, bead maker, and jewelry designer from Houston, Texas. She is inspired by nature, the colors and images of which can be seen in her earthy ceramic beads and pendants. Purchase her designs at *SpiritedEarth.etsy.com*.

Lyn Foley
Glass artist Lyn Foley designs jewelry using her unique handmade glass beads. She is also the author of *Go Anyway*, a book chronicling how she and her husband sold thriving businesses, their house, cars, most of their possessions, and moved aboard a sailboat. Her award-winning creations are sold at art shows and galleries in Texas and New Mexico and on her website, *LynFoley.com*.

Brandi Hussey
Brandi Hussey is a full-time artist inspired by color. She channels this passion into a variety of mediums, including jewelry, photography, and digital graphics. Find more information or connect with her at *BrandiGirlBlog.com* and *FreshlyHued.com*.

Libby Leuchtman
Libby Leuchtman fell in love with glass 15 years ago and the affair is still going strong. Making jewelry for nearly 20 years, she loves that she can create the beads for her designs. Libby teaches nationally. Find her beautiful beads at *LibbyLeu.etsy.com* and read her blog, *libbyleu.blogspot.com*.

Shannon LeVart
Shannon LeVart is a mixed-media jewelry artist who resides in Missouri. She wrecks metal on a daily basis and runs *MissFickleMedia.com*. She's also an author and contributor to books and magazines, and her unique patinated components have been seen in numerous publications.

Barbara Lewis
Barbara has pioneered the enameling of inexpensive steel beads, for a beautiful, cost-effective way to add color to jewelry. Her understanding of the effects of the flame on enamel is the foundation of her book *Torch-Fired Enamel Jewelry*. She shares her experience with artists who have a touch of pyromania at *PaintingWithFire.ning.com*. For more information, please visit *TorchFiredEnamelJewelry.com*.

Joanna Matuszczyk
Joanna Matuszczyk lives in Poland with her husband and three-year old son. She is a big fan of all things creative and has been a crafter and jewelry designer for since 2006. See her creations at *filcowe.blogspot.com*.

Melissa Meman
Melissa Meman lives in Frederick, Md. with her husband and son. She has been designing and handcrafting jewelry since 2002. Her eclectic jewelry and rosaries can be found at *MelissaMeman.com* or *MelismaticArtJewelry.etsy.com*

Sharon Palac
Sharon Palac is an English literature teacher as well as a published jewelry designer and metalsmith. She enjoys pounding metal, reading novels, baking cookies, camping, and relaxing with her husband, Walter, and their three rowdy canine companions. View more of Sharon's work at *SharonPalacStudio.etsy.com* and read her blog at *SharonsJewelryGarden.blogspot.com*.

Heather Powers
Heather Powers is an innovative bead and jewelry artist, creating art beads collected by bead enthusiasts all over the world. She is the author of *Jewelry Designs from Nature*, (Kalmbach Publishing Co. 2011). She teaches at workshops and retreats nationwide, and organizes an annual Bead Cruise. See her work at *humblebeads.com*.

Erin Prais-Hintz
Erin designs one-of-a-kind jewelry one piece at a time in her studio in Wisconsin, where she lives with her husband Paul and two children. Collaboration is the key to Erin's creativity and she enjoys nothing more than making connections with other artists and telling a story through her wearable art. Visit Erin at *Treasures-Found.blogspot.com* or *TesoriTrovati.etsy.com*.

Stephanie Sersich
Stephanie is from a family of artists and collectors and has been making jewelry since she was a child. While she works in many media, her jewelry incorporates a mixture of her own lampwork beads, vintage glass, ethnic beads, natural materials, and fibers. She teaches her bead-making and jewelry techniques all over the world. Her book, *Designing Jewelry with Glass Beads*, was published in 2008. Find her work at *sssbeads.com*.

Stefanie Teufel
Stefanie lives in Cologne, Germany. Her day job involves marketing a local newspaper, but her first love is to create and express herself. The vibrant colors of beads relax her and lighten her mood when she returns from work. She describes herself as a magpie with the urgent need to collect beads and fabric. Visit Stefanie by checking out her bi-lingual blog at *stefaniessammelsurium.blogspot.com* and her shop at *steufel.etsy.com*.

Cindy Wimmer
Cindy Wimmer lives in Virginia with her husband and four sons. She enjoys incorporating wirework with vintage components in her original designs. Cindy is the co-founder of ArtBLISS, hosting jewelry and mixed-media workshops in the Washington, D.C. area. Visit Cindy's website at *sweetbeadstudio.com*.

BASICS
Basic Jewelry-Making Techniques

Make a Plain Loop

1 To make a plain loop above a bead, trim the end of the wire to $3/8$ in. (1cm). Bend it at a right angle against the bead. To make a plain loop at the end of a wire, grasp the wire with chainnose pliers $3/8$ in. from the end. Make a right-angle bend.

2 Grasp the tip of the wire with roundnose pliers.

3 Gently roll the wire until you can't roll comfortably.

4 Reposition the pliers, checking that the fit is snug against the jaw, and continue to roll the loop. The tip of the wire should meet the corner of your initial bend, and you should have a perfect, centered wire circle.

Make a Plain-Loop Link

1 Cut a 2-in. (5cm) piece of wire. Follow the directions above to make a plain loop at one end.

2 String a bead or beads on the wire. Follow the directions above to make a plain loop above the beads.

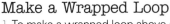

Make a Wrapped Loop

1 To make a wrapped loop above a bead, trim the wire $1\frac{1}{4}$ in. (3.3cm) above the bead. Grasp the wire with chainnose pliers above the bead. Fold the wire over the pliers into a right-angle bend. If you're working with just wire (no bead), grasp the wire about $1\frac{1}{4}$ in. from the end and make a right-angle bend over the pliers.

2 Switch to roundnose pliers. Position the jaws in the bend. Bring the end of the wire up and over the top jaw and as far down as possible.

3 Reposition the pliers so the lower jaw is in the loop. Slide the wire until is it snug on the jaw to be sure that you are working in the same place as in Step 2.

4 Bend the wire down and around the bottom jaw of the pliers until the tail is at a right angle to the neck of the loop. This is called "the first half of a wrapped loop." At this stage, you can connect the loop to another component, such as a chain link or bead dangle.

5 To finish the wrapped loop, switch back to chainnose pliers. Position the pliers' jaw across the loop, as shown. Use a second pair of pliers to grasp the wire at the end. Begin to wrap the end around the exposed neck. One wrap will secure the loop, but several wraps look nicer. Be sure to fill in the entire gap between the loop and the bead so the bead is secure. Trim the end and use chainnose pliers to press it close to the wraps.

Make a Wrapped-Loop Link

1 Follow the directions above to make a wrapped loop at one end of a 3-in. piece of wire.

2 String a bead or beads on the wire.

3 Follow the directions above to make a wrapped loop at the other end.

Open and Close a Loop or Jump Ring

1 To open a ring or loop, grasp it with two pairs of pliers held parallel to each other as shown.

2 Bring one pair of pliers toward you and push the other pair away from you.

3 String materials on the open ring or loop as desired. To close, reverse the Steps above.

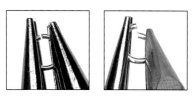

Make a Briolette Wrap

1 Cut a 3-in. (7cm) piece of wire, and center a top-drilled bead on the wire. Bend each side upward to form a squared-off U-shape. Leave a tiny bit of room for the bead to move—about 1mm.

2 Cross the wires into an "X" shape above the bead.

3 Use chainnose pliers to bend one wire straight up and one wire to the side. They'll form a right angle at their intersection.

4 Wrap the horizontal wire around the vertical wire as in a wrapped loop. Make two or three wraps and trim the wire.

5 Make a plain loop or a wrapped loop above the wraps made in Step 4 to create a briolette dangle.

Attach a Fold-Over Crimp End

1 Glue one end of the cord and place it in a crimp end. Use chainnose pliers to fold one side of the crimp end over the cord.

2 Fold the second side over the first and squeeze gently.

Make a Folded Crimp to Attach a Clasp

1 On flexible beading wire, string a crimp tube, a spacer, and half the clasp. Bring the wire end back through the beads just strung and pull on the end to tighten the wire.

2 Position the crimp tube in the notch closest to the crimping pliers' handles. Separate the wires, and firmly squeeze the crimp.

3 Place the crimp vertically in the notch at the pliers' tip.

4 Squeeze the crimp, folding it in half at the indentation made in Step 1. Check that the crimp is secure.

Make a Lark's Head Knot

Fold a cord in half and lay it behind a ring, loop, etc. with the fold pointing down. Bring the ends through the ring from back to front, then through the fold and tighten.

GROCERY LISTS
Bead Soup Project Resources

Bead Soup Soup
Toggle and chain from ADadornments.com; aluminum jump rings, TheRingLord.com.

Soup of the Day
Polymer clay beads, Heather Powers, Humblebeads.com; brass water lily component (P275) and toggle, Vintaj.com.

Ladle It Out!
Pendant, PalomaAntigua.etsy.com; hand-dyed silk ribbon, JamnGlass.etsy.com.

Zack's Watercress Soup
Pewter frog beads, GreenGirlStudios.com; toggle, ADadornments.com; hexagon spacers, Industrial Chic for Michaels, Michaels.com.

Summer Strawberry and Mint Soup
Bali silver beads, silver focal ring, SingarajaImports.com.

Soup in the Butterfly Garden
Jade flower button, FireMountainGems.com; copper filigree butterfly, ArtfulMarket.com; copper birds, Ornamentea.com.

The Key to My Heart is Good Cooking
Lampworked and silver heart, toggle, Cassie Donlen, GlassBeadle.com; vintage skeleton key, check vintage shops or etsy.com.

African Peanut Soup
Handmade lampworked pendant, beads, and headpins, Lyn Foley, LynFoley.com; wood washers, batik beads, large hole bead, BeadsbySandy.com; doe skin and suede, LeatherCordUSA.com

Chilled Blueberry Soup
Handmade sterling silver headpin, Lyn Foley, LynFoley.com; clasp, Erin Prais-Hintz, TesoriTrovati.etsy.com.

Vegetable Garden Soup
Ceramic bee pendant and beads, Nan Emmett, SpiritedEarth.etsy.com; polymer clay disk beads, Heather Powers, Humblebeads.com.

Shiitake Mushroom Soup with Citron and Lavender Sea Salt
Shibuichi pendant and clasp, SakiSilver.com

Waiter, There's a Ladybug in My Soup!
Stamped brass component, enameled beads, brass bead caps, Melissa Meman, MelismaticArtJewelry.etsy.com; ladybug pendant and earring disks, GolemStudio.com; antique brass filigree beads, ArtfulMarket.com; bronze clasp, IndoExpo.om

Portabella Mushroom and Carmelized Mushroom Soup
Lampworked focal and accent beads, Jennifer Cameron, GlassAddictions.etsy.com.

Stone Soup
Clasp, SweetBeadStudio.com; river rock pendant, RiverStoneBead.com; brass bird link, cmVision.etsy.com.

Cabin Fever Soup
Ceramic beads, toggle clasp, and owl pendant, Melanie Brooks, EarthenwoodStudio.com; lampworked beads, Jennifer Cameron, JenCameronDesigns.etsy.com.

Summer Soup
Lampworked Pod Focal bead, Libby Leuchtman, LibbyLeu.etsy.com; lamp-worked disk beads, Cassie Donlen, GlassBeadle.com; recycled glass African trade beads, BeadParadise.com

Bird's Nest Soup
Copper leaf, bird nest, earring wires, Sharon Palac, BijouxJardin.etsy.com; scribble wire beads, BeadsbySandy.com; bird focal, PalomaAntigua.etsy.com.; vintage acrylic polka dot bead, bluemarblebeads.etsy.com.

Handmade Soup Bowls
Lampworked focal bead, Kerry Bogert, KabsConcepts.com; enameled toggle, CKoopBeads.com; leather disk beads, BeadBreakout.com.

Blue Crab Soup with Chilies
Polymer clay donut, beads, and beaded clasp, Christine Damm, StoriesTheyTell.etsy.com; patinated charms, Shannon LeVart, MissFickleMedia.com; gemstones, sea bamboo, and Czech glass, LimaBeads.com; African recycled glass beads, TheBeadChest.com; Greek ceramic beads, LandofOz.com.

Blue Crab Earrings
Patinated copper rings, MissFickleMedia.com.

Ginger Peach Soup
Lampworked beads, FireLily.etsy.com; Bali tassel, SingarajaImports.com; sterling silver toggle, BeadGoesOn.com.

Twice Cooked, Twice as Good
Polymer fly pendant, purple faceted polymer bead, Barbara Bechtel, SecondSurf.com; filigree, Vintaj.com.

Version 2: Twice Cooked, Twice as Good
Polymer clay pendant, beads, and bird, Barbara Bechtel, SecondSurf.com; handmade sterling silver clasp, BeadSoupKits.com.

Fine Dining
Vintage earrings; hook clasp, Cindy Wimmer, SweetBeadStudio.com; rope chain, ADadornments.com; oxidized brass wire, jump rings, PatinaQueen.com.

Roasted Eggplant Soup
Wood pendant, wood beads, dyed Buri seeds, BeadsandPieces.com

Vintage Bean Soup
All patina beads and rings, Shannon LeVart, MissFickleMedia.etsy.com.

Silver Soup Spoon
Porcelain bird bead, SummersStudioEtc.etsy.com; polymer clay bead, Barbara Bechtel, SecondSurf.com; ceramic large-hole disk bead, DianeHawkey.com.

Golden Consommé of Acquitaine
Gold tassel, SingarajaImports.com.

Savory Tomato Soup
Lampworked beads, lampworked headpins, Kerry Bogert, KabsConcepts.com; pendant, clasp, RioGrande.com.

Soup at the Bistro
Thai silver tube bead, marcasite toggle, Zeelver.com; assorted Bali silver beads, Bali charm, IndoExpo.com; crimp tubes with top loops, RioGrande.com; Greek leather, LeatherCordUsa.com.

Fruit Compote
Fruit beads, LandofOdds.com; sterling silver curves, Shiana.com.

Blue Onion Soup
Lampwork glass beads, Libby Leuchtman, LibbyLeu.etsy.com; Kazuri beads, KazuriBeadsEast.com.

Autumn Harvest Soup
Enamel elements, chain, sari ribbon, bracelet blank, Barbara Lewis PaintingWithFireartwear.com; faceted abacus beads, toggle closure, Shannon LeVart, MissFickleMedia.com; copper leaf, rings-things.com; vintage copper flower SleepingDogStudio.etsy.com.

Old-Fashioned Oyster Stew
Vintage cameo pin, check vintages shops or Etsy; bronze toggle clasp, IndoExpo.com; brass puffy hearts, bead cap, chain, and headpins, BrassBouquet.com.

ARE YOU FULL YET?

As you've seen, there are so many different ways to put together beads, and trying out beads you never would have thought of using before can boost your designs, your excitement for the craft, and even your career.

Whether you follow the tutorials step by step or pick an ingredient here and there, I'm confident you'll find new paths to follow. As a largely self-taught jewelry designer, I've found the sort of methods I've described to be invaluable to my own seven-year design career. You're never too young or too old to try new things—and don't forget to keep thinking outside the box—or, the soup bowl.

Visit BeadSoupCafe.com, a thriving Facebook group for bead makers and jewelry designers alike. Learn about the next Bead Soup Blog Party at BeadSoupBlogParty.com, and join the fun!

SPECIAL THANKS

An enthusiastic, warm hug to my project designers and bead contributors for your outstanding designs, your patience and perseverance, your wonderful beads, and your shared excitement in this endeavor.

To Cindy Wimmer, whose beautiful bead bowl photography is so appreciated.

To Molly Alexander and Jennifer Brecht, whose early reading of the book helped me get things together.

To Rise Up Coffee, without whose coffee I would never have gotten this book written!

Special thanks to special sponsors: ADAdornments.com, ArtBeads.com, Golem Studio, and Urban Maille.

To Karin Van Voorhees, my editor, who believed in this book from its very beginning, and to all the wonderful people at Kalmbach Publishing Co.

And of course to the hundreds Bead Soup Blog Partiers over the years, whose creativity is awe-inspiring. Come join the party again!